Praise for *Trading from Your Gut*

"For all those who wonder if the powers of right brain thinking could apply to the trends-and-charts universe of stock and options trading, Curtis Faith has their answer. In *Trading from Your Gut*, Faith taps brain research, neurological models, and the wisdom of experience to provide a roadmap for decision making in a new era of volatility."

—**Daniel H. Pink**, author of *A Whole New Mind* and *Drive*

"I consider a book to be worth reading if it helps me develop a major paradigm shift. The section in this book about how to train your brain to help you become an intuitive trader blew me away and gave me some fantastic ideas that will significantly help traders learn to trade better. For me, that kind of idea-generating inspiration is what makes *Trading from Your Gut* a great trading book."

—**Van K. Tharp**, bestselling author of *Trade Your Way to Financial Freedom* and *Super Trader*

"Emotions are not tools of cognition. How we feel about a stock has no bearing as to how it performs. But with the skill of both a trained psychoanalyst and market pro, Curtis Faith's *Trading from Your Gut* examines the human instinct behind our investment decisions. Because we are too often our own worst enemy in the markets, this is a unique and thoughtful guide to overcoming the biggest hurdle of financial success...ourselves."

—**Jonathan Hoenig**, Portfolio Manager, Capitalistpig Hedge Fund LLC and Fox News contributor

"Curtis Faith's *Trading from Your Gut* pulls off a difficult task—extracting pithy, simple trading strategies from the complex world of behavioral finance and psychology. The author of the hugely successful *Way of the Turtle*—an essential read for any committed trader—Faith takes the insights derived from psychology, marries them to cogent observations by master traders like George Soros, and then superimposes them onto a series of analysis-based theories to deliver a cogent trading plan.

As Faith observes, reading this book should enable you to combine 'your smarts and your intuition,' all achieved with a left field combination of wisdom derived from Formula One racing drivers, skydivers, Napoleon Bonaparte, Roman military theory, and Jessie Livermore. Next stop? Combining quantum theory, the wisdom of Ben Graham, the genius of proper investing, and tips on how to survive volatile markets?"

—**David Stevenson**, FT's "Adventurous Investor" columnist

"From the start, Curtis Faith makes clear the difference between allowing emotions into trading and trading from the gut—emotion has no place in trading, whereas he asserts that your gut feelings can make the whole difference between mundane trading and master trading. Through a process of discovery, with many entertaining stories and examples, Faith explains his findings and leads the reader into developing a whole-brain approach to trading, utilizing both analytical and instinctual powers. With the encouragement of this book, you will learn to listen to both your intuition and your intellect to become a more complete trader, giving yourself the edge for success."

—**Alan Northcott**, author of *The Complete Guide to Investing In Short Term Trading*

Trading from Your Gut

Trading from Your Gut

How to Use Right Brain Instinct & Left Brain Smarts to Become a Master Trader

Curtis Faith

Vice President, Publisher: Tim Moore
Associate Publisher and Director of Marketing: Amy Neidlinger
Executive Editor: Jeanne Glasser
Editorial Assistant: Myesha Graham
Operations Manager: Gina Kanouse
Senior Marketing Manager: Julie Phifer
Publicity Manager: Laura Czaja
Assistant Marketing Manager: Megan Colvin
Cover Designer: Brand Navigation
Design Manager: Sandra Schroeder
Managing Editor: Kristy Hart
Senior Project Editor: Lori Lyons
Copy Editor: Krista Hansing Editorial Services
Proofreader: Apostrophe Editing Services
Indexer: Lisa Stumpf
Compositor: Nonie Ratcliff
Manufacturing Buyer: Dan Uhrig

Publishing as FT Press
Upper Saddle River, New Jersey 07458

Printed in the United States of America

First Printing December 2009

ISBN-10: 0-13-704768-1
ISBN-13: 978-0-13-704768-0

Pearson Education LTD.
Pearson Education Australia PTY, Limited.
Pearson Education Singapore, Pte. Ltd.
Pearson Education North Asia, Ltd.
Pearson Education Canada, Ltd.
Pearson Educatión de Mexico, S.A. de C.V.
Pearson Education—Japan
Pearson Education Malaysia, Pte. Ltd.

Library of Congress Cataloging-in-Publication Data

Faith, Curtis M.
Trading from your gut : how to use right brain instinct and left brain smarts to become a master trader / Curtis M. Faith.
p. cm.
Includes bibliographical references and index.
ISBN 978-0-13-704768-0 (hbk. : alk. paper) 1. Investment analysis—Psychological aspects. 2. Investments—Psychological aspects. 3. Speculation—Psychological aspects. I. Title.
HG4529.F34 2010
332.601'9—dc22

2009037199

For my two grandmothers,
Edna and Esther

Contents

Contents

Acknowledgments

This is my third book. You would think that after completing the first two, I would have a pretty good idea how much work is involved in putting a book together.

Except I keep forgetting. It's a lot of work.

My wife, Jennifer, helped me immensely with the manuscript. She helped me fix up my prose. She helped me with research. She helped me understand what was clear and what was fuzzy. The book is much better for her help. Thank you, Jen.

My superb editor, Jeanne Glasser, executive editor at FT Press, helped me with the initial concept for the book, she gave me frank criticism when needed and pushed me to make the book what it is. Thank you, Jeanne.

I would also like to thank Doug Coulter, Levi Freedman, Anthony Garner, and Jeremy Zerbe for their comments and review of the manuscript. Thank you.

Tim Moore, VP and publisher; Laura Czaja, public relations manager; Julie Phifer, senior marketing manager; and Amy Neidlinger, director of marketing and associate publisher at FT Press helped with the book concept, title, and marketing. Herb Schaffner, my publicist of Schaffner Media Partners, helped with marketing. Thank you.

Finally, I'd like to thank the heroes of production who turned these blank words into a real book: Lori Lyons, project editor; Krista Hansing, copy editor; Laura Robbins, illustrator; and Nonie Ratcliff, compositor. Thank you.

Foreword

by Van K. Tharp, Ph.D.

If I had relied on my initial instinct, you might not be reading this Foreword. You see, intuition is a concept with which I am quite familiar. I have a Ph.D. in psychology with an emphasis on biological psychology, so the first few chapters of this book did not initially capture my interest. Those chapters, however, are a great starting point for traders without a psychological background. I would suggest you particularly focus on judgmental heuristics and how they influence trading because they are so important to trading decisions. Some other topics of particular interest are covered in the first chapters of the book: the differences between the right and left brain, group phenomena and how they influence trading, neural networks and intuition, and the dangers of intuition.

One point that Curtis makes and repeats again and again in this book is that you must train your instinct to get the best results. Because I agree with that, I kept on reading—and I'm glad I did. Chapters 6 through 8 blew me away. In this section, Curtis shows you how to train your brain to help you become an intuitive trader.

Usually, I consider a book worth reading if it helps me develop a major paradigm shift. When I read this section of the book, I came up with some fantastic ideas that will significantly help traders learn to trade better. For me, that kind of idea-generating inspiration is what makes *Trading from Your Gut* a great trading book.

The final chapters of the book cover some important and general ideas related to trading and intuition: 1) Issues with backtesting and intuition, including some novel ideas on how to determine if a discretionary system is any good, 2) Balancing intuition and intellect, and 3) Living mastery.

Here's a quick look at different types of intuition and how my trader coaching experience has proven to me why intuition is invaluable.

Despite all of the advances in computers over the past 50 years, no computer comes close to a human brain. For example, I like to trade efficient stocks (stocks that trend with very little noise or random movement). A straight line going up at a 45-degree angle would be a perfect example of an efficient stock; however, I've never see one that looks that good. Most trending stocks show a lot of whipsaws, which I define as representing the amount of noise in the movement. The following graph is a fairly good example of an efficient stock. It's LQD, the long-term bond ETF, since last march. It just keeps going up with very little noise.

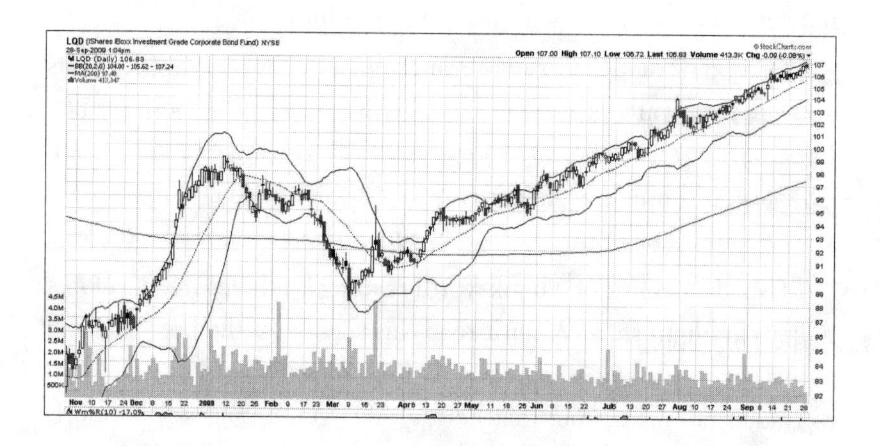

No matter how hard I've tried, it's been nearly impossible to program software that will give me a list of the most efficient stocks. The best I have been able to do is to compile a list of stocks to screen. I still have to look at the price chart of every stock to find the efficient ones. Anybody's brain can easily pick out an efficient stock just by looking at it, whereas a computer cannot. Trading such visual price patterns is often called *discretionary trading*, and that's the first form of intuition.

The second form of intuition helps us with lots of data. The amount of information to which our brains are exposed just about doubles each year, especially since the advent of computers and the Internet. Your conscious mind, however, can handle only about seven chunks of information—plus or minus two chunks. To understand what that means, try this simple exercise. Have someone call out a long list of numbers while you have your hand raised. When you can no longer remember all the numbers called out, lower your hand. Unless you've mastered some advanced memory techniques, you probably will remember only about five to nine numbers—right in the range of normal human capacity. But what happens when you are exposed to thousands or even millions of chunks of information? You develop some judgmental heuristics (mental shortcuts) to cope. There are many famous heuristics that have been documented by psychologists over the past 20 years, and Curtis does a good job of documenting the role of these heuristics in trading.

A third form of intuition develops from thoroughly understanding a task and bringing lots of experience to it. Somehow, people with such experience do a superb job of sensing opportunity or danger quickly when no one else can imagine how they did it. Somehow, traders who have developed this kind of intuition just know that the market is about to turn down and can get out quickly. Alternatively, some can sense when a massive opportunity is about to occur. John Templeton, for example, used much of his fortune to short dotcoms at the beginning of 2000. Through the late 1990s, many were in agreement with Templeton basic logic: The dotcoms' business models did not merit their lofty stock prices. Applying that logic and shorting the dotcoms six months earlier, however, meant those traders either had to cover their shorts at a loss or suffer through huge drawdowns. Templeton's timing was impeccable. How did he know when to short the dotcoms? Intuition. Similar feats have been accomplished by others in 1929, 1987, and at other major market turning points. The timing was absolutely amazing, and the only explanation for these feats is intuition.

In a more personal example, I worked through some deep psychological processes with a retired engineering professor in 1994. As a result of that work together, he connected with his internal guidance. Over the next 15 years that guidance directed him in many different directions, including trading. In 1994, he already had a substantial trading account but by mid-2008, he had grown it by 5100%. And then his guidance told him to stop trading—right before the 2008 market meltdown.

I spent some time with him in mid-2008, and he showed me exactly how he traded. In fact, it is surprisingly similar to my preference for efficient stocks. It was sound, logical, and very simple. He looked at the top five industry groups for long stocks and the bottom five industry groups for short stocks. The first step involved intuition. He could generally review a list of stocks and based upon volume, accumulation, and a few other variables, he could tell which charts from that group he needed to look at.

When he finished his initial screen, he looked at stock charts in two different timeframes: 1) a year's worth of daily bars and 2) 30 days worth of hourly bars. His charts included two simple moving averages, momentum, plus DMI+ and DMI-. He couldn't tell me exactly how he entered positions except to say that the price needed to be above both moving averages in both timeframes. I got the impression that he often looked for a short-term retracement in price to the short-term moving averages and then a bounce back.

When did he exit the position? My impression was that he exited when the price reached the longer term moving average. When I asked him about his exits, though, he totally flabbergasted me. He said, "I've done this so much that I can look at a chart and pretty much tell how long the stock will keep moving up—whether it's going to be several months or just a few days." "How?" I asked. He said, "I don't know, I just can tell." That is the power of intuition.

So here was one of my better clients with whom I had worked to clear out enough psychological issues that he could plainly hear and follow his internal guidance. That guidance directed him toward this sort of trading. Then, with experience following his guidance, he developed intuition in two additional ways. First, he could just tell when to enter into a position. Second, and more impressive, he could just look at the chart and have a pretty good idea of how long it was going to be moving in his favor. That is superb intuition, which helped him produce a 5100% return in 14 years. After trading for that period of time with those kinds of returns, he listened to his internal guidance unquestioningly in early 2008 when it told him to stop trading. Although he was proficient at shorting, I suspect that this final guidance saved him a lot of money.

You, too, can learn how to develop that kind of intuition by reading this book. Amazingly, developing your intuition and understanding the benefits for your trading psychology are the very kind of ideas that most traders want to pass over. They want facts and computerized methods that "work." My experience of nearly 30 years as a trading coach, however, has clearly demonstrated that you cannot become a superb trader based purely upon mechanical trading methods. Intuition is an integral component of the success for the best traders in the world. Keep that in mind as you read *Trading from Your Gut*.

Van K. Tharp, Ph.D.
NLP Modeler and Trading Coach
www.VanTharp.com

PREFACE

Zen and the Smooth Stroke

"I learned to approach racing like a game of billiards. If you bash the ball too hard, you get nowhere. As you handle the cue properly, you drive with more finesse."

—Juan Manuel Fangio

I grew up with a pool table in my basement, so I learned to play at an early age. As a kid, I could beat most of my friends because they didn't have the chance for practice like I had. I could also usually beat my father, who had taught me the game, because he didn't play as much as I did. So, in my own small universe, I got to think of myself as a pretty good player.

I wasn't.

At some point long after I left the house, my father started playing in pool tournaments at the local billiards hall near where he worked. It didn't take long before he was good to the point that I almost never won a game when we played. I went from being able to beat him pretty consistently to being totally outclassed. It was clear that I didn't know as much about playing pool as I thought I did.

Several years later, after I left the software company that I had started, I found myself with a lot more free time; so, I decided that I would learn how to be a good pool player. I followed my father's path and showed up to play in the local weekly pool tournaments in Reno, Nevada, near where I lived at the time.

Reno is a serious pool town. The United States Pool Players Association (USPPA) even holds its annual amateur nine-ball tournament in Reno. The best players from all over the country come each year to play.

As a practical matter, the presence of all these great players meant that I lost most of my games. Decisively.

I was used to playing eight-ball games with the occasional straight-pool game thrown in. The tournaments were generally nine-ball tournaments, so I had to learn a new game. In nine-ball, you have to hit the balls into the pockets in consecutive order. The object is to be the first one to get the nine-ball into the pocket. So you first hit the one-ball, then the two-ball, and so on, until you get to the nine-ball. The first player to sink the nine-ball wins.

When you first start to play pool, you think that the object is to get the ball into the pocket. So you spend a lot of time worrying about aiming the ball and hitting it into the pocket. After a certain amount of experience, you get to be pretty good at pocketing a ball if it is not too difficult a shot. At this point, you also come to realize that the trick is not sinking individual balls; the trick is making sure you don't leave yourself too many difficult shots. This is especially true in nine-ball, where you are permitted to hit only one ball at any particular point, and then the next ball, in order.

So the key to nine-ball is controlling where the cue ball goes after it hits the target ball. The real aim isn't hitting the ball into the pocket—that's a given. What you need to do is not just drop the numbered ball, but also control where the cue ball stops so you can set up for the next shot. To do this, you need to learn how the way you hit the ball affects the path of the cue ball and to develop control over your shot. Acquiring this skill takes a lot of practice. A good nine-ball player makes each shot seem effortless because the cue ball lines up after each shot to make the next shot easy.

In pool, the act of hitting the cue ball with the pool cue is called the "stroke." A smooth, accurate stroke is the foundation of good pool play. I learned this while getting absolutely crushed in hundreds of games with some very good players. If you have a smooth stroke, the cue goes straight and the ball goes where you aim it. If you don't, then the aim won't matter. If you have a smooth stroke, you can predict where the cue ball will end up. If you don't, you can't.

For me, the key to having a smooth stroke was not over-thinking the shot. After hundreds of hours of practice, I generally knew what to do. If I spent too much time thinking prior to taking my shot, I found that I would often force the stroke and miss the shot slightly. Sure, the ball might even go in, but I'd leave myself with a poor following shot. If I played the shot with my head, I would end up miss-stroking the cue ball.

After a while, I found that I got better—not because my knowledge of what to do improved; not because my feel for the shots improved; but because I became more comfortable with just shooting without thinking. I learned to trust my gut instincts.

As I began to trust my intuitive game, I began to play more consistently. I stopped over-thinking shots, and my stroke was more consistent. I'd learned the smooth stroke.

Over the years, I have noticed that over-thinking can harm performance in other areas. In particular, I have seen many traders paralyzed by putting too much emphasis on the rational analytical decision process. Many traders don't perform at their full potential because they only use part of their mind—the analytical and linear conscious mind of the left-brain hemisphere. They use their intellect but not their intuition.

They do this because they have not learned to trust their gut instinct and their intuition.

If you want to trade at the level of a trading master, you need to develop both parts of your mind—your smarts and your intuition. I'm not the first one to suggest this idea. Many of the world's most famous traders have said this before me. They were correct.

Although there are many books about trading analysis and techniques for the analytical mind, there is a lack of books about developing trading intuition. That's why I decided to write this book.

In *Trading from Your Gut*, I show how to develop your intuition and confidence in the decisions of your gut instinct so that you can use your whole mind while trading.

CHAPTER 1

The Power of the Gut

"The intuitive mind is a sacred gift and the rational mind is a faithful servant. We have created a society that honors the servant and has forgotten the gift."

—Albert Einstein

George Soros, one of the greatest traders alive, trades from the gut. He has widely remarked on the correlation between his backaches and trading choices. In the autobiographical *Soros on Soros,* he wrote:

> I rely a great deal on animal instincts. When I was actively running the fund, I suffered from backache. I used the onset of acute pain as a signal that there was something wrong in my portfolio. The backache didn't tell me what was wrong—you know, lower back for short positions, left shoulder for currencies—but it did prompt me to look for something amiss when I might not have done so otherwise.

Some traders might scoff at the idea of making decisions based on "feelings" or intuition. They see the trader's role as one who remains calm and collected, rationally choosing the right course while those around them are tossed about by their emotions. They believe that Soros is either lying or fooling himself. They don't see how gut instinct can help. Yet many successful traders feel otherwise. Who is right? Is one approach better than the other?

If you are one of those traders who doesn't believe that gut instinct or intuition has any place in trading, I invite you to keep an open mind. I, too, once felt as you did. After all, I was trained to take a very systematic and logical approach to trading as a Turtle. I believed that it was important to keep your emotions in check. I didn't believe in trading from the gut.

Trading from your gut is a way of tapping into the extra power of the right hemisphere of the brain.

What I didn't realize at the time, however, is that there is a big difference between trading emotionally and trading from your gut. Trading emotionally means reacting to fear and hope, which can destroy your trading decisions. Trading from your gut is different. It is a way of tapping into the extra power of the right hemisphere of the brain, which can be a powerful, effective, and entirely rational addition to any trader's repertoire.

Trading comes naturally to some people, as it does to Soros or my trading mentor, Richard Dennis, for example. They seem to have a knack for it that comes from a well-developed sense of intuition. This gut intuition can be developed through training and the right kind of experience. In this book, I teach you how to incorporate expert-level gut instinct in your trading.

Before I go further, it is important to further define exactly what I mean by **intuition** and **gut instinct**.

Intuition

In mid-November 2007, when the Dow Jones Industrial Index was above 13,000 and the S&P 500 Index was above 1,450, I attended the Trader's Expo conference in Las Vegas, Nevada. The Trader's Expo is the largest trading conference in the country; people come from all over the western United States to attend the conference. I had been invited to speak at the conference in conjunction with the publication of my first trading book, *Way of the Turtle.*

While I was at the conference, I was asked to do an interview with MoneyShow.com, which had set up a video recording studio in one of the conference rooms. The interviewer asked me what I thought of the markets over the previous several weeks. Normally, my standard response is that I don't try to predict the markets. I had grown weary of giving advice and had found that specific advice is not generally useful to others when not considered in context.

This time was different. I decided to go out on a limb and advise that viewers be very cautious in their stock investments. I told them that I thought there was a higher than normal chance that the markets would go down a significant amount, that we were coming off a long period of steady gains, and that there was a good chance we had seen the end. The timing was prescient. It turned out to be the beginning of the downturn that would see the market lose more than 50% of its value over the next 16 months.

You may think my instinct had told me that the market would soon decline. This is only partially true. I thought the market was risky at that moment, for some very specific reasons that had nothing to do with my instinct as a trader. Where my intuition came in was in breaking my longstanding rule not to talk about what I thought might or might not happen. I just had a feeling that this time was different, that I should voice my concerns.

If you asked me, I could probably come up with some reasons I felt obliged to share my thoughts on the direction of the market, but these reasons would be somewhat contrived. The truth is, I didn't really know why I spoke up; I had an intuition, a gut feeling, but one without a logical basis that I could readily articulate. In fact, the rational side of my brain was arguing for me to keep quiet because I knew that predicting market movement was a fool's game. In retrospect, I hope that sounding this early warning benefited the traders who saw the video.

Using Gut Instinct: Left Brain Versus Right Brain

Relatively recent advances in psychology and neuroscience show that human intuition can indeed serve as the basis for powerful rapid decision making. Our brains can make decisions using thousands of individual inputs almost instantaneously. This type of rapid parallel processing occurs in our right-brain hemisphere. Because of the speed of the right brain, it can be a powerful tool in the hands of an experienced trader. Unfortunately, too much reliance on an untrained gut can prove disastrous for the inexperienced trader. This makes proper training very important.

Analysis, linear thinking, ordering, and the need to find structure dominate left-brain thinking. We try to make sense of the world with our left brains and bring order to it. We categorize, theorize, rank, and file with our left brains. When you think out loud, you are using your left brain. Put another way, when you think *consciously*, you are using your left brain.

The right brain, in contrast, is concerned with the whole picture and the spatial relationships between each of its parts. The right brain is quick and intuits instead of reasons. If you've ever felt uncomfortable or unsafe but couldn't pin down the reason, this was your right brain's sense of intuition generating that feeling. The right brain excels at reading patterns and interpreting their meaning in the context of a larger picture, and it moves much more quickly than its counterpart.

Although the right brain can quickly come to a conclusion or recognize danger, it cannot generally explain the reasons why it has arrived at that conclusion.

This speed comes at a price. Although the right brain can quickly come to a conclusion or recognize danger, it cannot generally explain the reasons why it has arrived at that conclusion. This often puts it at odds with the left brain because that analytical part of the brain wants explanations for its decisions.

To better understand how the right brain works, it's worth looking at the processes embedded in neural networks.

The Artificial Brain: Neural Networks

In the 1970s and 1980s, researchers in computer science attempted to re-create the brain's function using simulated neurons connected through computer software. They created the first artificial neural networks. As research in neural networks continued, this technology proved to be excellent at recognizing patterns. However, the downside of neural networks was the same as that of the right brain and the speed at which it arrives at conclusions. Neural networks can rapidly reach conclusions, but it is impossible to examine a neural network to understand the assumptions it is drawing from.

The right brain works a lot like a neural network. It draws upon experience to reach suppositions, but we generally don't know the reasons for those conclusions, except as a feeling. So if the left brain wants to explain and the right brain cannot offer explanations, which side wins in a battle of decision making?

The answer depends on personality.

Thinking Versus Feeling: Can't We All Just Get Along?

Psychiatrist and pioneering psychologist Carl Jung developed a theory that measured one's personality in three different areas. In each area, individuals had a personality that fell somewhere on a continuum between one extreme and the other. One of these is a continuum between thinking and feeling; scores on a test of this personality aspect measures the extent to which the right brain or the left brain dominates decisions.

Isabel Briggs-Myers and her mother, Katharine Cook Briggs, subsequently developed Jung's work. Their work has been popularized as Myers-Briggs personality types. The Thinking and Feeling axis (generally abbreviated as T or F) of the Myers-Briggs test is often equated with rational decision making and emotional decision making. Sometimes those who make decisions using their left brains (the T's) look at those who make decisions with their right brains (the F's) and think that the F's are being unreasonable when they cannot explain exactly why they make particular decisions.

Most schools are geared toward developing and training the left brain. Math, science, reading, writing, and rote memorization are all left-brain activities. This emphasis leaves some would-be traders with a relatively overdeveloped left brain and underdeveloped right brain.

A balance between left-brain analysis and right-brain intuition is critical for optimum trading.

A balance between left-brain analysis and right-brain intuition is critical for optimum trading, so training must overcome any disparity a trader has in his cerebral development. Every trader has a dominant hemisphere, but recognizing the nondominant hemisphere is also important, especially if this is the right brain.

The Two Trading Camps

Consider another way in which the fight between the left and right hemispheres affects trading, in the ideological battle between discretionary (gut) and system (left-brain) approaches. The trading world is divided into two fairly distinct camps. The largest camp consists of traders who consider trading an art, those who are called **discretionary traders**. A smaller group consists of traders who use a specific set of rules to make their trading decisions. These traders are known as **system traders**.

Often when traders first meet each other, they ask if the other trader is a discretionary or system trader. For most successful traders, the answer is rarely black and white, because trading styles generally fall on a continuum between the purely intuitive discretionary trader and the purely rule-oriented system trader. Individuals who think of themselves as discretionary traders range from shoot-from-the-hip traders who buy and sell when it *feels* right, to more methodical traders who use combinations of chart patterns and mathematical indicators to trade only when a set of conditions have been met. Investors who think of themselves as system traders range from traders who use such a specific set of rules that they can be programmed into a computer, to those who use a loose set of rules in combination with their own ability to recognize certain patterns and market conditions.

The best discretionary traders tend to be right-brain dominant, using their intuition to decide when to make trades. This tendency is especially prominent among discretionary day traders who look to profit from small intraday price movements. For these traders, the speed of their decision making is often a critical factor if they are to be successful. They might describe their approach as having a "knack" for the market or a "feel" for the direction of the market.

Left-brain traders know exactly why they put on certain trades. They generally have a very specific set of criteria that must be met before they initiate a trade. In contrast, purist right-brained traders, who use their intuition almost exclusively, often don't understand exactly why they make certain trades; they just know when a trade feels right. This willingness to relinquish decision making to intuition or gut characterizes the hard-core right-brain trader.

System traders are most often left-brain dominant. They use a rational, systematic process to decide when to make trades. They often analyze their approach using computers to perform "what-if" analyses using historical data to determine the hypothetical results their trading methods might have earned in the past, a process known as **backtesting**. Left-brain traders don't trade on their gut or intuition; they trade using rules and strategies. These traders often think in terms of signals and triggers, as specific events that determine when to initiate a particular trade. Systems traders will have identified these specific criteria earlier, when they performed their backtesting and historical analyses.

Whole-Brain Trading

After reading my first trading book, *Way of the Turtle,* which lays out a very rational approach to trading, some readers might think that I believe left-brain trading is better or more valid than intuitive right-brain trading. I don't. Even though I got my trading education as a Turtle in a tradition that stressed a systematic approach to trading, I see plenty of value in the right brain's ability to quickly process lots of information to arrive at an intuitive conclusion. In short, both approaches have merit.

Whole-brain trading involves both hemispheres and is a balancing act between the brain's two primary types of cognitive function: logical reasoning, and intuitive feelings and impressions. The blend of right brain and left brain depends on the type of trading you are involved in. For extremely short-term trades, relying on the right brain is often the only practical approach. Traders simply do not have enough time to perform complicated analysis. Traders who are scalpers must trade mostly using their right brains. For longer-term trading, traders have plenty of time for analysis. Getting historical data for performing this analysis also is relatively easy. Therefore, longer-term trading is very suitable for the left-brain trader. **Swing trading**, in which trades are kept for a few days or a few weeks, is best addressed with whole-brain trading. Generally sufficient time exists for performing an analysis, but the data and tools available to the typical trader do not generally permit a completely systematic approach such as one might use for long-term trading. For this reason, whole-brain trading is virtually required for effective swing trading.

In this book, I show discretionary traders how to strengthen their intuition and gut instinct and how to incorporate analytical tools that systems traders traditionally use. I also show systems traders how to use many of the tools and techniques that discretionary traders use, to develop more robust trading methods. My approach to trading, and the philosophy that I share with you in this book, is what I refer to as **whole-brain** or **whole-mind trading**.

Mastering the Art of the Trade

To become a master trader, to be able to intuitively make good decisions, you must first gain enough of the right kinds of experience. This is why doctors and nurses go through extensive training and supervision when they are new to the profession. It is why firefighters train in fire simulations, and why airline pilots train in flight simulators. Through this constant exposure and consistent practice, experts build up a library of experiences that they can draw upon when making decisions.

To become a master trader, to be able to intuitively make good decisions, you must first gain enough of the right kinds of experience.

The same holds true for the trader—the most effective training is trading itself. In this way, the experiences you encounter while trading train your intuition so that, in time, you can become an expert. Learning as a trader can be difficult, however, because of the price of mistakes. In trading, mistakes cost money. Fortunately, traders can develop their intuition to a high level of expertise without having to put their money at risk. I discuss several strategies for doing this in upcoming chapters.

Before I lay out these strategies, it is important to understand the pitfalls and dangers of relying on gut feeling and intuition if you have not yet received proper training. In the hands of a novice, gut instinct can be dangerous to your account balance. In the next chapter, "The Purpose of Gut Intuition," I cover this important topic.

CHAPTER 2

The Purpose of Gut Intuition

"Intuition will tell the thinking mind where to look next."

—Jonas Salk

One of my Turtle friends still suffers from partial paralysis after having been infected with the polio virus as a child in the early 1950s. Polio was the biggest killer of children in those times, and many who didn't die were left paralyzed.

The whole world looked to science for a cure. Researchers had identified the virus in 1908, but for more than four decades, a cure remained elusive. So it was an important event on April 12, 1955, when Jonas Salk announced the results of the first clinical trials of a promising treatment. His polio vaccine was effective and powerful.

Most of the other polio researchers had been working on vaccines that used live viruses. They did not believe that a dead virus could be effective. The trials for these live-virus vaccines had proved dangerous because they infected the subjects with the very disease they were trying to inoculate against. Several of the trials resulted in the deaths and paralysis of children, so the live-virus vaccine proved not much safer than the polio virus itself.

Why had Jonas Salk decided to buck the trend and use a dead-virus vaccine when this approach had never been used? It all started with his intuition—a feeling that something just didn't make sense.

More than 20 years before his successful vaccine, while Salk was still in medical school, he had attended two lectures that influenced him greatly. He still remembered them more than 50 years later. During the first lecture, he learned about immunizing against diphtheria or tetanus bacteria using chemically treated or dead versions of the bacteria. During the second lecture, he learned that humans had to experience viral infection itself for immunization against a viral disease. The lecturer said that science could not induce immunity with an inactivated or dead virus.

In his gut, Salk knew something didn't make sense. If you could use a dead bacterial toxin to immunize people, he thought, you ought to be able to use a dead virus to immunize them as well. So 20 years later, when the most prominent researchers were using live viruses, Salk trusted his earlier gut instinct and continued to work on a polio vaccine that used a deactivated virus.

Salk's intuition paid off. His vaccine worked. A live-virus vaccine wasn't deemed safe enough for general use until 1962—seven years after Salk's vaccine was approved. Tens, perhaps hundreds, of thousands of people were saved from contracting polio because of Salk's intuition.

The best purpose of gut intuition is to keep us from wasting time on the wrong approach and to keep our conscious, rational mind focused on what is important.

As noted in the earlier epigram, the best purpose of gut intuition is to keep us from wasting time on the wrong approach and to keep our conscious, rational mind focused on what is important. If you learn to listen to your gut, as Salk did, you, too, can find success. But you need to be careful.

The Dangers of the Gut

Although gut instinct and intuition can be powerful tools for success in the hands of an expert, they can prove dangerous for the less experienced trader. One reason is that these individuals often approach trading with certain prejudices and tendencies that are counterproductive or just plain wrong, such as placing too much weight on the news. This practice creates certain assumptions about the future price direction for a given stock based solely on one's gut reaction to the news. The problem with this sort of intuitive judgment is that the very premise on which it is based is flawed: The news is not the source of market movement. It does not shape markets, and thinking so takes an overly simplistic view of a very complex landscape.

A trader who starts with the flawed premise that one can predict market price movement with an analysis of the news is going to have problems. A flawed premise combined with intuition still leads to a flawed outcome. The outcome is only as good as the foundation upon which it is built.

Inexperienced traders commonly latch on to a particular trading guru's methods. These new traders often follow the guru's explanation for how to trade without bothering to build an internal rationale or model for why those methods will work. They follow the letter of the law without attempting to understand the spirit of the law. They attempt to learn the "what" but not the "why" for trading based on a particular method. The problem with this approach is that it is static: It can't adapt to changing markets. It also leaves no room for the gut.

The best approach is to use each part of our brain for what it is best suited to. The left brain is good at building and understanding models for how the world of trading works, and the right brain is good at generating ideas and recognizing opportunities.

For the right brain's intuition to work to one's advantage, it must be primed with a full set of scenarios from the left brain that provides the proper context. If the context is flawed, the resulting intuition will be imperfect as well.

The left brain is good at building and understanding models for how the world of trading works, and the right brain is good at generating ideas and recognizing opportunities.

This explains why master traders use their whole mind for trading. They prime their right brains with patterns that their left brains understand and categorize using carefully reasoned analysis. Analysis supports the intuitive process and ensures unbiased thinking by giving traders enough mental models for them to make sound judgments. Analytical thinking also performs an evaluation and ranking function that is critical for "training" intuition.

Getting Your Brain to Listen to Your Gut

To better understand how to train intuition, let's look at the process used for developing neural networks. Neural networks simulate the connections between neurons in the brain and are a mainstay of artificial intelligence in computer science. Neural networks are excellent at categorizing and recognizing patterns, but, as in humans, this is a learned skill.

To recognize patterns, neural networks first need to be trained. This process involves submitting sample data to the neural network representing the patterns that you want it to recognize. The training rewires the neural network to reflect the knowledge required to understand the pattern presented.

What do I mean by *knowledge* in this specific case? If you think about the process your brain uses to determine if a piece of furniture is a chair or a stool, you can get some idea of how your brain uses knowledge. Your knowledge about chairs and stools is the information you use to determine whether some new piece of furniture is a chair, a stool, or neither. Specifically, this knowledge includes the traits the two types of furniture hold in common: that both a chair and a stool are something you sit on. The knowledge also includes the concepts that differentiate a chair from a stool: that a chair is of a specific height to fit a typical table and generally has a back, whereas a stool has no back and is generally either shorter than a chair and used for stepping to reach high objects, or taller than a chair and used for sitting at a bar.

In a neural network, the knowledge consists of idealized models that are categorized according to domain-specific categorization schemes (or **taxonomies**), as well as the relationships among and between those models. The picture that springs to mind when you think of the word *chair* is an example of an idealized model. What you use to differentiate a chair from a stool is an example of your brain's knowledge of the relationship between the idealized chair and stool.

The neural network "learns" by being exposed to new examples and the values for their hierarchical place within their particular categories. For example, you might feed the neural network a picture of ten chairs and tell it that these are chairs, ten stools and tell it that these are stools, and ten tables and tell it that these are tables. This process enables the neural network to build internal models of what these examples represent. After the training, the network has internal models that represent its knowledge of the differences among chairs, stools, and tables.

Taxonomies are categorization schemes. If you were building a character-recognition neural network, one set of categories would be the letters individually, as well as the set of uppercase letters and lowercase letters. A given example might be categorized as a letter *A* and also separately as an uppercased letter. Another example might be categorized as a letter *c* and a lowercase letter. A perfect neural network contains enough knowledge of the requirements for each category to be able to determine whether a new sample fits the category. The knowledge required to determine membership in a given category is known as a **model**.

Much as you don't generally picture a specific chair in your mind when you think of the word *chair,* the models that a neural network builds don't represent specific letters that you have encountered. Instead, they represent the idealized forms for each letter. The model for the English letter *S* is the idealized curved shape of the letter; it is similar to how you envision the letter *S* in your mind. For a neural network to recognize an *S* in an arbitrary typeface, the model it contains must be sufficiently complex so that it can distinguish between an *S* and the other letters. The model can't be too specific, or it won't be able to distinguish among an **S** in the Cambria typeface, an **S** in the Comic Sans MS Bold typeface, and an **S** in the Sante Fe LET typeface. For the neural network to function properly, the model contained in its neural connections needs to capture the essence of the letter in an abstract sense.

Consider what would happen to the neural network if it was presented with the number 5. Would it be able to distinguish between the letter *S* and the number 5? It depends on the sophistication of the model. If the model incorporated the concept that the number 5 has sharp angles in the top with soft curves on the bottom, and the letter *S* has soft curves on both top and bottom, then the model would incorporate enough knowledge to be able to properly distinguish between them.

Training a neural network to properly distinguish between *S* letters and 5 numbers requires examples that incorporate the characteristics that distinguish between the two symbols. If a neural network has been trained with examples of only letters and no numbers, then it will not be able to distinguish between *S* and 5. The choice of examples must be sufficiently broad for the training to be effective.

The choice of what examples to feed to a neural network and the ranking for how well each of the examples fits with the model is a left-brain activity. The left brain also analyzes the complexity of a particular problem and makes assessments of potential models. For example, the left brain would analyze the similarities between *S* and 5 and realize that at least one extra layer of complexity in the model is required to distinguish between these similar characters. The neural network's pattern recognition is a right-brain activity. After using examples to configure and train a neural network, it can automatically recognize patterns and perform categorization. In a computer or in the human brain, it can do this almost instantaneously.

The left brain is good at extracting abstract models from patterns and examples, and at establishing and choosing categories. The right brain is skilled at determining whether a given example fits the model that defines a category and is good at recognition. *The left brain analyzes and the right brain notices.*

The left brain analyzes and the right brain notices.

Whole-Mind Learning

In the human brain, these functions build on each other, with each half taking its turn and then passing off the results of its function to the other hemisphere. Let's now consider how beginning traders learn about trading patterns.

Figure 2.1 represents the ideal or model for the double-top pattern. It shows a significant rise in price, then a pullback, and then another rise in price that reaches the same level as the previous top. This will be the pattern that traders have in their heads when they think about the double-top pattern.

The Double-Top Pattern

FIGURE 2.1 The double-top pattern

Now look at Figure 2.2. Each of the three examples in this figure is similar to the model for the double-top pattern, but each differs in an important way. Examples A and B show an initial top followed by a second, higher top. Examples C and D show an initial top followed by a second, lower top.

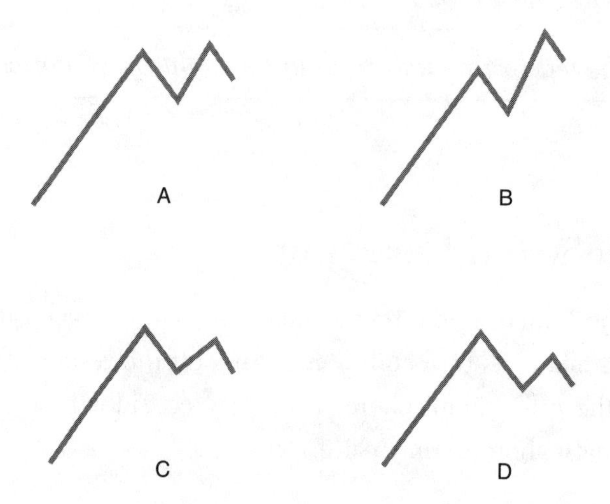

FIGURE 2.2 Potential double-top patterns

For traders who have been supplied with only a description of the idealized double-top model, it is not easy to determine which of these examples might be a valid double top. That is because they do not understand why a double top is important, nor do they understand the implications of the price movement on the psyche of the market participants. Therefore, it is difficult for such traders to decide whether a particular price formation that does not exactly fit the model is indeed a double top.

Much as the neural network must be trained by sample data with associated category ranking, human intuition must be trained with examples and an associated valid ranking. The examples and their rankings that you have in your mind must be sound for the resulting intuitive analysis to be valid. For example, if you don't have a good idea of what represents a double top, you won't be able to intuitively assess the presence of a double top in the future. Your right-brain intuition is only as good as the training it receives. People need to use both the left and right brain to learn. You need the ranking and analysis of your left brain to make sense of the patterns you use to train your right brain. With the correct analysis and mental framework from your left brain in place, your right brain will be able to do what it does best: recognize patterns and situations.

When master traders use their whole mind to trade, they alternate between analysis and ranking from left-brain and right-brain intuition in a cyclical fashion. Optimal learning involves a continual iteration between the two hemispheres. For example, as traders execute new trades and gain more experience, they will continuously notice patterns in trade performance and market pricing using their right brains, and these patterns will cause them to have questions. They will then use their left brains to formulate ways of answering those questions that will likely include tests, analysis, and linear thinking that the left brain is very good at. However, during this process, the right brain will have plenty of opportunities to take notice; this might bubble up to the surface of consciousness as a feeling that a particular pattern being presented is important, and the left brain will then try to rationalize this feeling. If the left brain is unable to do so, left-brain-dominant people will often discard the feeling as irrational. However, right-brain-dominant people will pay more attention to the feeling; they might even act on it without an explicit rational, linear, left-brain reason.

Traders who use their right brains will be more creative and will develop more novel ideas because of their willingness to act on feelings without an explicit rational reason. This can be very beneficial during trading research when the rationale for a particular trading idea or pattern might not be obvious ahead of time. The feeling that an idea will pan out gives the right-brain trader sufficient will to perform the often tedious work of cold analysis required to validate a trading idea using the left brain.

Traders who use their right brains will be more creative and will develop more novel ideas because of their willingness to act on feelings without an explicit rational reason.

At the same time, inexperienced right-brain traders are susceptible to acting on ideas based on feelings drawn from erroneous principles because they have not sufficiently trained their right brain in proper trading principles. They have not yet supplied the right brain with enough of the raw material required to make proper judgments. For this reason, the gut reaction of the novice trader will often be wrong.

The Primitive Gut: The Importance of Honing Your Instincts

One of the reasons that the novice's gut reaction is often wrong stems from the shortcuts that come preprogrammed into human minds. Our minds reflect the evolution of our ancestors, who selected for beneficial traits. Often the very traits that served human beings well in the primitive past do not serve us well as traders. The shortcuts that are preprogrammed into our brains are called **heuristics**. Several common heuristics, called **cognitive biases**, cause traders to make systematic errors in judgment. Through proper training, traders can learn to overcome these biases.

I learned the importance of overcoming systematic errors in judgment during the first month of trading as a Turtle when we were all given a small trading account. My intuition correctly told me that the most important factors would be how well we displayed the spirit of our training, took advantage of the opportunities that arose, managed our risks, and handled the trading on an emotional level. Most of the other Turtles thought our goal was to make as much money as possible during that month—to have the highest account balance possible.

My gut told me otherwise. If a trade came that met our criteria, I took it no matter how risky it seemed. I was concerned with performing well on my own terms, not making money, per se. My intuition paid off. A trade in heating oil seemed like a very risky trade when it started, so risky that many of the other Turtles missed it. In doing this, they displayed a bias known as *loss aversion*. I took the trade because my intuition told me it was the right thing to do, despite the risks. That trade turned out to be a big winner. It was probably the most important trade of the entire Turtle program because, on the basis of that first month of trading, I was given the largest trading account among the Turtles, a distinction I held for the duration of the four-year program.

It wasn't my smarts that made me take that trade, and it wasn't my left brain. All the Turtles were smart; they all knew enough to see that the heating oil trade met our criteria for entry. The difference was intuition: I followed my gut instinct.

CHAPTER 3

Wrong-Brain Thinking

"Nothing is more intolerable than to have to admit to yourself your own errors."

—Ludwig van Beethoven

I first learned about trading from my employer when I was a high school senior. It was not only my first job as a computer programmer, but it was the first job I had in which I used my brain instead of my body.

My first task was to translate computer code that my boss, George, had written for the Apple II computer. I translated the Apple version of the BASIC computer language into the version that ran on the relatively new Radio Shack TRS-80 computers. I spent my time coding each statement one by one; at first I didn't pay much attention to what the code actually did. However, I soon learned that the code I translated read information from of a set of files that was in a specific format for the floppy disk. These files contained pricing data for commodities such as corn, wheat, gold, and silver. Then the code performed some math and simulated buying and selling commodities contracts.

After I finished the translations, I was assigned the more interesting job of programming new trading algorithms from the then-new 1980 book by Charles Patel, *Technical Trading Systems for Commodities and Stocks.* This was my first introduction to the world of systems trading. I liked the idea of a trading system. It seemed like a scientific approach to extracting profits from the markets. Yet I couldn't shake the feeling that trading systems seemed too good to be true. "It can't be that easy," I thought. My intuition was partially right. Many of the systems we tested were crap; they didn't make any money. But some of the systems made quite a bit of money according to the testing programs I was running at work.

Livermore demonstrated that money could be made in the markets because the nature of the people trading never changed.

About the same time that I started programming the code for trading systems, George lent me a copy of Edwin Lefevre's book *Reminiscences of a Stock Operator,* introducing me to the great speculator Jesse Livermore. I was hooked. I decided that I wanted to be a trader. What really interested me was the way Livermore demonstrated that money could be made in the markets because the *nature* of the people trading never changed. For example, he said, "The game does not change and neither does human nature." This was my first introduction to the idea that money could be made in trading because of the way that human nature interacted in groups.

George lent me other books that greatly influenced me: Charles Mackay's 1841 classic *Extraordinary Popular Delusions and the Madness of Crowds* and Gustav Le Bon's 1895 classic *The Crowd: A Study of the Popular Mind.* These books started me thinking that some trading systems or algorithmic strategies seemed to work because they relied on repeatable market-price patterns based on the consistency of human nature over time.

I refined this perspective after studying psychology. I learned how the actions of groups of traders influence price in repeatable ways. If you want to understand these repeated price patterns, you first need to consider why most traders lose money—to recognize the behavior of the majority of traders.

One of the commandments of the master trader is that if you want to make money trading, you can't *act* similar to most other traders, but you need to *know* what they are doing. Instead of using their right brain, they use their "wrong" brain. In this chapter, I explain why they lose money and delve into what "wrong-brain thinking" means.

Brain Science

Neuropsychology has taught us that the physical structure of the brain is prewired with certain tendencies designed for survival and reproduction of a species. These tendencies or instincts function similarly to a series of prime life lessons that are with us when we are born and that the brain applies opportunistically. These prime lessons are also referred to as **cognitive biases**, and some would suggest that these biases represent faulty thinking processes. This is incorrect. In most circumstances, cognitive biases are very useful. However, in specific limited scenarios—particularly in trading and finance—they can trip you up.

To become a master trader, you need to retrain your gut to override cognitive biases in specific trading circumstances. Traders also need to understand these cognitive biases to avoid **herdthink**. When you've gained control over your cognitive biases, you can choose the appropriate course of action: anticipating the herd, doing the opposite of the herd, or avoiding any action while the herd panics.

In the next few sections, we explore some of these prime lessons or biases, along with the specific trading behaviors that each lesson precipitates.

Gun-Shy: He Who Runs Away Lives to Fight Another Day

The instinct for avoiding unnecessary risk can be very powerful. This is a trait that ensures survival under conditions of danger and uncertainty. When deciding whether to risk getting eaten by a crocodile, a lion, or another dangerous animal, humans needed to minimize risk as much as possible. The rule "Better safe than sorry" makes sense for most people most of the time. Driving at a prudent speed, eating a healthy diet, keeping in shape, using child seats in the car, and avoiding unnecessary risks pay off in longer life expectancy.

But in trading, avoiding risk will prevent you from becoming a good trader, let alone a master. Traders trade in risk; it's that simple. Master traders view risk as an important and necessary ingredient in any potential trade. They know that the very best trades are often the ones that are hardest for most people to make because of the perceived high risk. The very fact that a trade is difficult to initiate makes it less likely that others will also make that particular trade. The lack of a large number of traders taking a similar position makes it much easier to make money during the subsequent price movement.

News and Noise: Listening to What Matters

Your brain wants to save energy and storage, so sometimes it takes shortcuts. One of the most common and useful instincts is the shortcut of ignoring the details in a complex picture by focusing on and retaining only a few specific points. The brain's sensory-perception system is architected to do this. People have three kinds of memory. **Sensory memory** lasts from milliseconds to seconds and holds information from the senses that the perception system then processes. The perception system uses **working memory**, lasting from seconds to minutes, and sorts and filters information that cognitive systems need to process. Your cognitive systems are consciousness and attention. These systems process the information from our perception system, discarding anything unimportant and retaining key information or anything that it believes might be useful later in **reference memory**, which lasts for hours, days, or years. Much of the time, your visual perception system is processing and then discarding most of what you see. Your working memory holds on to images that are noteworthy—things you find especially interesting or novel, things that might harm you, anything that presents opportunities for food or mating, and anything that might affect your social standing. All these types of visual images represent, either directly or indirectly, the images that are most likely to affect your ability to survive and procreate.

If you overload the sensory system, it will go numb and start to ignore the signals it receives. This is one of the reasons 24-hour financial news channels can be so harmful to traders. *Too much data exists, and much of it is irrelevant.* The financial news programs create the illusion of market movement when nothing significant has happened, in order to have something to report. They build the story and reasons behind the market going up or down even when the market moves up and down in only meaningless amounts.

Most of the time, the markets are not doing anything that merits our attention.

The perception system is designed to look for outliers, the standouts. If you spend too much time listening to news channels or reading the wrong blogs and Twitter streams, you can start to lose the ability to distinguish the standout from the noise. Most of the time, the markets are not doing anything that merits our attention.

Your perception is normally very good at filtering signal from noise. One of the more interesting examples that illustrates this point is a person's ability to tune out noise to focus on a single conversation during a cocktail party or at a large table at a restaurant. Scientific studies have shown that, to your mind, the conversation to which you are paying attention appears louder than it actually is, sometimes as much as three times louder.

However, if the noise is too loud, your perception system cannot distinguish among the different conversations, and you will have trouble focusing on your own conversation. The noise will overstimulate your sensory system and cause it to function less efficiently. The same thing happens when you overstimulate your perception system by watching the markets too closely, watching financial news incessantly, or obsessing over every tiny up and down the market makes. Master traders have learned to pay attention to what is important and to ignore noise. Your brain is naturally good at this if you train yourself to not overstimulate it.

If you get bored waiting for something significant to happen, you should do something else while waiting for the market. Trading can certainly be exciting at times, but it is not entertainment. Don't treat it like it is. Sometimes doing nothing and being patient is the right thing to do. As Jesse Livermore famously said, "The market does not beat them. They beat themselves, because though they have brains, they cannot sit tight."

Mental Inertia: La De Da, La De Da

At the height of the Internet bubble, I was working in Silicon Valley. In those exuberant times, I was amazed at the almost universal perspective that the good times would never end. Most of my friends were heavily invested in stocks, many of them trading on margin. They believed that the Internet had changed the world of finance and that the stock market would only go up. I saw the same perspective in the real estate and stock markets of 2006 and 2007. Many people believed that the bull markets were here to stay. They could come up with all sorts of reasons why this time was different and why prices would continue to go up. I didn't share their opinion. I had seen my share of bubbles and crashes; I knew that the market tended to change when people, especially the public, least expected it. The events that have taken place since summer 2008 prove this point.

Master traders are always ready to change their opinions and perspectives. They consistently look for the reasons why they are wrong instead of trying to prove themselves right. Master traders don't suffer from mental inertia.

Mental inertia comes from the prime lesson that new learning is retained for later use. When you form an opinion, it takes some specific impetus to change that opinion. The stronger your opinion, the stronger the impetus required to change that opinion. So when you have an idea that the market is not good for buying, it takes considerable motivation to change that idea. When a trader decides to place a trade, it often takes considerable drive to change course and exit the trade.

Mental inertia results from a mismatch between the decisiveness required to act and the strength of the opinion required to make those decisions. Your brain wants sufficient data before making a decision; when it has that data, it requires significantly more information to change its mind.

The mental inertia of individual traders and investors causes the markets themselves to act similar to a heavy object. Have you ever tried to push a stopped car on a level road? It can be very hard to get it rolling; when it gets rolling reasonably fast, it can be very hard to stop—especially because the power brakes don't usually work when the motor isn't running, which is usually the case when you have to push a car. Most market participants are too slow to react to significant changes in the markets. They are too slow to get in when an opportunity presents itself, and they are too slow to get out when the opportunity ends. They don't want to give up losing positions or ideas. If they are convinced that a particular stock is going up for some reason, they will hold on to that idea even when the price drops. If they buy a stock and it starts to go down, they will convince themselves that they are correct, despite the market's overwhelming evidence to the contrary.

Master traders know that mental inertia is one of the major reasons behind market momentum. They also know that, because of this inertia, the best time to get in is right before most other traders enter the markets, and the best time to exit is just before most other traders exit the markets. Because they understand the inertia of markets and the mental inertia of the market participants, they look for signs that the markets have begun to react to some external force just before anyone else takes notice.

Master traders also look for places to enter the markets with trades that offer a good risk/reward opportunity. They determine these places by using an assessment that incorporates mental inertia of market participants as part of the model.

Keeping What's Yours

The prime lesson or instinct for avoiding loss makes sense in more traditional circumstances. It takes effort to acquire any possessions: grain, cattle, sheep, shelter, and other items. We should safeguard and protect possessions that require work to acquire. Novice traders naturally try to avoid losses, which is one of the main reasons they focus on **high-percentage strategies**. They want to have many more winning trades than losing trades, so they focus on anticipating the market and trying to predict its direction.

As I mentioned earlier, I am generally reluctant to comment on the market's direction. Instead of trying to predict the markets, I focus on what it is *doing now* and what that means. The problem with prediction is that you can be very off with the timing. You can be right and still lose a lot of money because the market might take a long while to arrive at the same place. However, if you know what the market is doing right now and what it has done in the past, you can find times when the odds of the market moving a significant amount tip in your favor. Taking a trade is not the same as making a prediction. Master traders often take trades that they believe are more likely to result in a small loss than a gain based on their knowledge of past market movement. How much money they will make over time is the important factor, not how often they are correct.

A related problem new traders have is that they often look at losing trades as bad trades. This is related to their desire to predict. Their built-in circuitry equates losing with bad and winning with good. This evaluation is certainly correct over many trades and the long term, but it is an incorrect assumption in the short term. Master traders recognize that losing is a cost of doing business. They also recognize that the markets often reward behavior that is psychologically difficult for most traders to exhibit or manage. Trading strategies that are difficult to follow are usually significantly more profitably than those that are easy to follow.

Many new traders use easy-to-follow strategies, especially ones that seem obvious. Consequently, these strategies tend to work for only a brief period of time. Usually they stop working as soon as enough traders have started to follow them. Therefore, the desire to avoid losing trades can be a major disadvantage.

Master traders know that the percentage of their trades that make money is not as important as the amount of money they end up with. A few large winning trades can easily offset many smaller losses. Therefore, master traders often look for trading strategies that have many small losses and relatively few larger winners.

The long-term, trend-following trading style we used as Turtles is one example of this type of trading strategy. In one year that I was up more than 200%, I had perhaps 10–12 winning trades and 45–50 losing trades. The winners were big (5%, 20%, 40%, or more) and the losing trades were all small (0.5% losses). If you were trying to predict the market, you would have been better off taking the opposite of my trades.

You need to learn to be comfortable with losing money if you want to trade successfully.

Many master traders have learned to substitute the idea that losing is always bad with the strategy of cutting losses short and letting winners run. Losses are part of trading. You need to learn to be comfortable with losing money if you want to trade successfully.

Another way that the prime lesson for avoiding losses can trip up traders and other market participants—who think of themselves more as conservative investors than as traders—is in the tendency to avoid facing reality when presented with mounting losses. Many market participants watch their losses mount thinking that they aren't really losses unless they sell their stock. They hope that the market goes back up so they don't have to "book" their losses. In behavioral finance, this is called **loss aversion** or the **sunk cost fallacy**.

These same traders and investors often reach the point of despair later, when they get tired of watching continued losses mount. This commonly happens at the worst possible time, when many others are also selling in panic. This sort of behavior is usually what lies behind the extreme drops in price that accompany major bear markets. First, many people ignore reality as the price falls, until finally the decline is large enough that they can't ignore it any longer. Then panic sets in, making the price drop even further and triggering more panic.

Master traders don't have a problem booking losses, so they don't sit by and watch small losing trades develop into major losing trades. They get out while the loss is small, and they don't view it as a bad decision. They know that losing trades are a natural part of trading.

When we Turtles were first given our trading accounts, we were allowed to pick between two different styles of stop losses for our entries. The more common approach was to put a stop loss at twice the average trading range for a given commodity. An optional approach was called the **whipsaw**. Richard Dennis told us that the whipsaw performed better but was much harder to do because it meant many more losses. After each loss, you might need to reenter the market again if it went back in the opposite direction. For example, if you bought gold at $400 and the average daily range was $10, you would place your stop at $380 under the normal exit approach. But using the whipsaw approach, you would get out if the price dropped to $395. If the price dropped to $390 and then rose again to make a new high, any of the Turtles who traded using the whipsaw approach would get out at the stop price and then get back in again when the market rose.

I traded using the whipsaw approach, even though I knew it would be harder to do, because I wanted to trade based on the strategy that Dennis's analysis had shown to perform best in historical testing. This meant that a higher percentage of my trades were losers, compared to trades made by the other Turtles who did not use the whipsaw approach. It also meant that my average loss was lower than theirs. Over time, I believe that my strategy was more profitable—perhaps 15% to 30% a year better, depending on the year.

If at First You Don't Succeed: The Importance of Persistence

One of the more powerful instincts our brain exhibits is persistence: You should persevere even in the face of difficulty and obstacles. Dogged persistence usually pays off. It enables you to reach difficult goals and accomplish great tasks. Most of science's discoveries would likely not have occurred if human brains had not been programmed to persist in the face of adversity.

For traders, persistence is both required and problematic. Persistence will carry you through the difficult times when the inevitable losses come, when your account draws down from its highs, and when the markets are not friendly. Unfortunately, persistence can also cause many traders to stick to methods that don't work or to stay in a trade they should have exited long before. This behavior is especially problematic because it is often combined with mental inertia. Traders might place a trade for a specific reason. Mental inertia will prevent them from seeing the mounting evidence that the reasons for the trade are no longer present and that they should get out. Persistence will move them to persevere, shouldering the pain of the mounting losses in an effort to achieve the goal.

Master traders have learned to reverse course quickly, understanding that they should not keep enduring losses. Persistence in pursuit of the long-term goal of profits is important. Persistence in a particular trade can sometimes result in more harm than good.

See, I'm Right: Hubris, Damned Hubris

A behavior that has caused problems for many traders is the desire to find supporting evidence for previously held decisions or ideas, and the tendency to overlook contradictory evidence. This tendency is called **confirmation bias** in behavioral finance. Traders need to pay attention to reality instead of wishful thinking. The best approach is to play devil's advocate and troubleshoot those ideas or decisions, to identify where they might be wrong.

One of the more interesting concepts I have heard in the last few years is the notion that wisdom is the capability to have "strong opinions, weakly held." My favorite financial blogger, Barry Ritholz, first brought this concept to my attention in a post in which he described how he thought it applied to trading and investing. The concept originated with Paul Saffo from the Palo Alto Institute for the Future, a nonprofit organization that helps companies make decisions about the future. Saffo applied the concept to the uncertainty associated with making forecasts about the future. The idea has considerable merit in any area with a high level of uncertainty, such as trading.

Weak opinions have a negative impact on trading. Master traders are decisive. *To make money, you need to take trades.* As a practical matter, this means developing models for how the market works, testing them, and then making live trading decisions using those models. Traders need strong opinions about how the market works to make critical trading decisions. Many people have trouble pulling the trigger. If you have weak opinions, you will find this even more difficult.

However, strong opinions should be weakly held. Expert traders are constantly on the lookout for why their thinking might be flawed. When you place a trade, you should pay far more attention to signals that the market is acting in a manner that indicates the trade is wrong and should be discarded than to the reasons why the trade should be kept. As the saying goes, you should speak and act as if you are right, but also look and listen as if you might be wrong. In circumstances of high uncertainty, you should always be looking for indications that your previous ideas are wrong. This requires a certain level of humility and openness.

Good Decision, Bad Outcome

The brain is not designed to process the type of low-probability outcomes that traders often encounter, where losing is part of the game.

Perhaps the most insidious instinct for traders is the brain's tendency to equate the quality of a decision with its outcome. The brain is not designed to process the type of low-probability outcomes that traders often encounter, where losing is part of the game. Therefore, new traders will often make a trade, lose money, and then think to themselves, "I shouldn't have made that trade." In behavioral finance, this tendency is known as **outcome bias**.

Master traders know that any particular trade could be a losing trade and that good trading strategies often bring losing trades. Therefore, they have learned to undo the effects of this outcome bias and to focus not on the outcome for a trade, but instead on the quality of the decision behind the trade.

Right-brain-dominant traders have an advantage in this area. The right brain naturally focuses on the big picture—the forest instead of the trees. This is the correct approach when examining a series of trades. The big picture matters—the effect of a large number of trades. The individual trees don't matter except in how they contribute to the overall forest.

Left-brain-dominant traders will find it harder to retrain their instinctual tendencies toward this bias because their nature encourages them to logically evaluate every trade on an individual basis to determine whether it was good or bad. Traders can't really make this sort of evaluation. Individual trades are neither good nor bad. Only when the trades are considered in aggregate can any sort of evaluation be made—and that evaluation is not of the trades themselves, but of the strategy that produced them.

What Have You Done for Me Lately?

The brain's perception system weighs recent data more heavily than data that preceded it. In behavioral finance, this tendency is called **recency bias**. This is a temporal instinct. In trading, this tendency is responsible for some of the patterns that emerge in price charts. (We demonstrate this in greater detail in the next chapter.)

Although the most recent prices are sometimes important, focusing solely on the most current information to the exclusion of all other data creates problems for market participants. This tendency can often magnify the effects of mental inertia. Mental inertia will cause many traders to discount the rise in price as indicative of anything significant. This will make them less likely to want to buy. A focus on recent pricing will cause many traders to view the new prices as "high" in relation to recent prices.

Because many traders, especially new traders, don't like the idea of buying when the price is "high," they avoid trades at relatively high prices. They want to buy when prices are "low" and sell when prices are "high." Master traders consider the recent past but do not weigh it more than is justified. Therefore, they have no problems buying when others consider the price "high" or selling when others consider the price "low." Master traders also understand how this tendency to focus too much on the recent past can cause other traders to miss opportunities and to react too slowly during major market shifts.

Follow That Herd

One of the mental shortcuts that our brains are programmed to make is the belief that doing what others are doing is safer than doing something different. Human beings are social animals. We take cues from others in our social circle. This tendency is a mental shortcut that saves us valuable effort. In a small tribe or band, following others makes good sense. It serves as the basis for much of our learning. We learn by following the example that others set. We learn what foods are good to eat by eating what others eat. We learn our culture. We learn our preferences.

Marketers have used this tendency to increase demand for their products, knowing that consumers take their cues from prominent individuals. That's why the use of celebrity endorsements is so effective. We have no logical reason to care what kind of car Tiger Woods drives, but we are nevertheless influenced in our purchase decision by that knowledge.

This tendency, which is known as the **bandwagon effect** in finance, causes major problems for traders who are not aware of how it impacts the market. Too many people jumping into a market almost always results in bubbles and busts. The stock market bubble of 2000, the real estate bubbles of 2003 and 2007, and the oil and commodities bubbles of 2007 and 2008 were all caused by too many people jumping on the bandwagon at the same time.

Master traders don't make trades because others are making them. They make trades for their own specific reasons. They look to get aboard before bubbles develop, and they are quick to exit at the first sign of trouble. However, those who get caught up in herd mentality join the bubbles long after the market starts rising. Then they exit only when the herd itself exits, which is after the bubble has burst and all the profits have dissipated with it.

If you want to be a master trader, you need to develop your own reasons for making trades.

If you want to be a master trader, you need to develop your own reasons for making trades, and you need to avoid doing anything just because others are doing it. Independence of mind and spirit is one of the hallmarks of a master trader.

In the next chapter, I explain how groups of market participants exhibiting the instinctual behaviors outlined in this chapter create repeating market phenomena.

CHAPTER 4

The Structure of the Markets

"There is no logical way to the discovery of these elemental laws. There is only the way of intuition, which is helped by a feeling for the order lying behind the appearance."

—Albert Einstein

I often find that I learn something about one domain when I'm least expecting it. Sometimes it happens when I'm working on something altogether different, such as playing chess.

One of the clearest memories I have of the Turtle days, especially the first year when I spent every trading day in a room with the other 11 Turtles, was my surprise at being around so many smart people with such varied backgrounds. Each of us had one or two areas in which we really excelled.

One Turtle, Mike Cavallo, was a very good chess player. He was so good that he could easily beat me without even looking at the board. I was by no means an expert, but I considered myself a decent player. The fact that someone could beat me while playing the game in his head was humbling. I wondered what enabled him to so easily beat me and keep track of the pieces of the board in his head without breaking a sweat.

I have always had a series of open interests, areas I intend to learn something about. The list changes as I become competent at some things and discover new areas of interest over time. Learning to fly an airplane and to skydive have been on the list; flying a helicopter still is. Cavallo caused me to add chess to that list.

I continued to improve my game during the last decade because of a street player in New Orleans who sets up his board on the route between the convention center and the French Quarter. Every few years, I end up at a convention in New Orleans and I run into the same guy. He sits on the sidewalk at night offering to play anyone for a $20 bet. Every time I've come upon him, I've played a game. So far, I have always lost.

Learning enough to eventually beat him keeps chess on my list. As I have improved, our games have been closer. The last time we played, I had him on the defensive and almost beat him, only to make a rookie mistake at the end and lose.

As I've moved about the country and the world, I have continued to study and practice chess. I have revisited the basics many times—I found that each time I did so, I learned something new. Ultimately, my game has improved to the point that I could on occasion beat the president of the chess club I belonged to in the Virgin Islands. After years of practice, I finally learned how to play a competent game of chess, and I have developed an insight into how Cavallo was able to play masterfully without looking at the board.

It was the structure of the game: the way the pieces and positions all hung together, the causal sequence of events, the signs of strength and of weakness, the need for patience, the importance of striking only when an advantage presents itself, and the need for simultaneous defense and offense.

As with the moves of a chess master, the master trader makes trades with purpose and precision.

The markets have structure, too. Similar to a good chess player, a master trader doesn't just make trades in isolation. The trades are made in the context of the master strategy and the state of the markets. Some markets call for defensive trades. Some markets call for patience. Others call for aggressive persistence. As with the moves of a chess master, the master trader makes trades with purpose and precision.

My chess game had always been intuitive. Even early in my game, I could see the clever moves; I could find the combinations to work my way out of trouble, and I could often exploit weaknesses mercilessly. But I had no sense of how to put the odds in my favor, how to exploit weakness when the signs of that weakness were hardly visible, and how to put pressure on the opponent to force mistakes. Intuition alone was not enough. I needed to understand the structure to place my moves into a strategic context.

Repeating Price Behavior

Having gut intuition in trading is not enough to become a master trader. You also need a mature understanding of the structure of the markets, or as Einstein said, "a feeling for the order lying behind the appearance." This implies the use of the whole mind—a mix of the analytical left brain and the intuitive right brain.

In a 1991 interview with The Academy of Achievement, Jonas Salk highlighted the need for both hemispheres:

> Reason alone will not serve. Intuition alone can be improved by reason, but reason alone without intuition can easily lead the wrong way. The[y] both are necessary. The way I like to put it is that I might have an intuition about something, [so] I send it over to the reason department. Then after I've checked it out in the reason department, I send it back to the intuition department to make sure that it's still all right.

To be able to check out intuition, we need our left-brain reason to supply the proper structure and framework. In trading, this framework's foundation is the repeating market-price behaviors that stem from the repeated interactions among market participants. People, namely traders and investors, react similarly under similar circumstances; their behavior repeats in predictable ways. When you aggregate a large group of people into a market, this repeated behavior shows up in the form of repeating market-price movements.

Repeating market-price behaviors are the source of all trading profits because they present the opportunities to gain an edge in trading. An edge is a slight statistical advantage over random behavior. For example, if you can identify market price behavior that makes it statistically just as likely that the price will go up $1 in the next few days as that it will go down 50¢, then you can make a trade to buy that stock and, over time, you will make money. Each time you trade, you will have a 50/50 chance of losing 50¢ or winning $1 per share. The profits from a small edge averaged over many trades add up quickly.

Identifying these repetitions is not easy—otherwise, making money trading would be child's play. Master traders understand the importance of this skill and use a combination of right-brain instinct and left-brain smarts to identify and benefit from repetitions in market behavior.

I discussed the scientific names of several cognitive biases in the last chapter, and I gave you a quick look at how these biases impact trading. In this chapter, I go much deeper into the subject of trading psychology. I cover the psychological underpinnings of five concepts that are core to the structure of trading: price, momentum, cycles, support and resistance, and euphoria and despair.

Before you can correctly identify the repeating opportunities that signal an edge, you need to understand the building blocks of the structure itself. This might seem too basic for some readers, but have patience. Remember, I learned to play a decent game of chess only after I bit the bullet and spent years revisiting the basics that I felt I, too, already knew.

What's in a Price?

At any given point in time, price represents an equilibrium point: the balance between buying and selling dynamics. It also reflects a spillover of psychological pressure.

At any given time, the market generally contains buyers who want to buy at lower prices and sellers who want to sell at higher prices. In an ordered market such as the NASDAQ Exchange, these prices are made explicitly by the individual market participants placing orders. A buyer might place an order to purchase 100 shares of Google (GOOG) at a price of $400 or less. A seller might place an order to sell 100 shares at $420.

If these traders are the only buyer and seller, their orders would make up the bid and ask. The price would be quoted as $400 bid, $420 ask. The **bid** is the highest price that a buyer is willing to pay, and the **ask** is the lowest price at which a seller is willing to sell. At any given point, a bid and an ask exist for each market. (Generally, the difference between the bid and the ask, known as the **spread**, is very small—not $20, but more like 1¢ for a liquid stock such as Google. I am using large spreads to make the concept easier to read and understand.)

> *For a trade to take place, someone somewhere must capitulate.*

For a trade to take place, someone somewhere must capitulate. If the buyer is more anxious to buy, his anxiety will spill over into his order, and he will place either an order above the market or a market order that will have him paying the current asking price. In this case, the seller who created the offer represented by the ask price wins and gets her order filled. She sells her 100 shares at $420, the price she wanted.

When a buyer and seller are willing to trade at the same price, this results in a deal. The price of this trade will be what a quotation system lists as the last price. Using our GOOG example, the buyer using a market order will end up paying the $420 price, and the seller will sell her shares of GOOG at that price. The buyer capitulates by using a market order and ends up paying the higher price at $420.

It is possible for the bid and ask to remain the same while the price bounces up and down between the bid and ask. A trade taking place at the ask means that at least one buyer has capitulated; trading at the bid means that at least one seller has capitulated.

Normally, the bid and ask are very close together, so this is a minor capitulation; in liquid stocks, the difference between the bid and ask is generally a penny or less. So for many traders, the capitulation is minor. They want to get their trade filled quickly and don't mind paying the extra penny on a buy or losing the extra penny on a sell. However, sometimes capitulation can be dramatic when very large spreads arise between the bid and ask.

Spreads widen during times of uncertainty. If the market starts swinging wildly or takes a sudden plunge, the spreads widen. This happens because the traders who are looking to make only small trades earning some portion of the spread move the prices at which they are willing to buy and sell to account for the increased uncertainty of market direction.

This problem is generally most noticeable during price drops. If the market takes a sudden plunge, the price drop itself will cause potential buyers, those who might have been thinking of buying, to reconsider and wait. They wait for two reasons. First, they know that if the price continues to drop, they will be able to buy at a better price. Second, the price drop itself might have signaled a change in market conditions. Because every trade is made using an assumption about the condition of the market, a price drop might remove the very reason that a trade may have been a good idea in the first place.

Ironically, a trade at a higher price is sometimes a better trade. Dramatically lower prices often signal a significant shift in psychological power between buyers and sellers and a mass capitulation of the sellers. Many sellers entering the market from a psychologically weak perspective can depress prices for a significant period of time. At such times, it often makes sense to wait until equilibrium is restored.

Understanding that price is a psychological phenomenon is key to understanding the structure of the markets.

Understanding that price is a psychological phenomenon is key to understanding the structure of the markets. When you see price movement on the charts, you are looking at movement in the aggregate psychological perspective of the market participants.

Market Inertia and Momentum

Markets display inertia similar to physical objects. It takes some force to start them moving in a particular direction, and after they are moving, they tend to keep moving. Markets at rest tend to stay at rest, essentially bouncing about a certain range. Markets that rise tend to keep rising, and the same is true for descending markets.

Market momentum is derived from the underlying psychology of the market participants. It is the result of a chain reaction, a contagion of belief and perspective. This contagion requires an initial trigger, but when an epidemic of buying or selling reaches a certain point, it creates a reinforcing feedback loop. Buying creates more buying, which creates even more buying. Selling brings more selling, which begets even more selling.

Momentum in the markets is similar to a brush fire during the dry season. It takes only a little spark to start things burning, and then it becomes a self-sustaining phenomenon. The fire will slowly grow as it reaches progressively larger brush. Eventually, it reaches a point at which the heat from the fire is so high that it takes less time for the flames to spread. The heat also creates an updraft that brings in fresh oxygen and further raises the heat, creating a self-sustaining feedback cycle. Fires that have reached a certain threshold burn out only when fuel runs out or rains come. The amount and character of fuel present often dictate the character of the fire itself. If the underbrush is thick, the fire will burn hotter and faster. If the underbrush is very dry, it will catch fire more easily and also burn hotter and faster.

Markets are much the same. Uncertainty is similar to the hot, dry air that dries out the brush, and anxiety, fear, and greed are similar to the grasses, brush, and trees that spread the fire. The greater the price movement, the more uncertainty that movement will create in the minds of those observing it. An individual trader will be less sure that he can predict what the market will bring after it moves in an unexpected manner. If he has no position in the market, this increased uncertainty will likely keep him from entering the market. If he has a position that was harmed by the movement, his fear will increase.

Similar to the smaller twigs and grasses in a brush fire that are easily set aflame, some traders reach the point of panic or fear more quickly and more easily than others. So when the market drops suddenly, some traders will react fearfully, worried that they won't be able to sell. These traders will sell using market orders, which is a trader's way of saying, "I don't care what price I get—just get me out." They panic.

This panic drops the price further because the "sell at market" orders result in trades at the bid price, which during a sudden price decline is invariably at a price significantly lower than the last trade. The bid drops far below the asking price because the level of uncertainty of both the future price and direction of the market increases during sudden market drops. The greater the uncertainty, the larger the spread between bid and ask. In fact, this is one of the ways you can measure the uncertainty implied by the market's pricing. A spread widening substantially indicates greater perceived uncertainty in the market participants.

When the spread is wider after a sudden price drop, a market order will result in a relatively greater drop in the price. And a group of market orders placed at about the same time will result in a large price drop, illustrating how uncertainty acts like the fuel for a brush fire. If a lot of uncertainty exists, you'll see much greater market swings.

Similar to a brush fire, market momentum stops when it has exhausted its fuel of fear, anxiety, and greed.

Similar to a brush fire, market momentum stops when it has exhausted its fuel of fear, anxiety, and greed. As with a brush fire that burns grasses and small shrubs but does not catch the large trees on fire, some market panics are relatively small. Others, like a brush fire that reaches the canopy of trees, spread to more seasoned traders—those who are less prone to panic. Momentum takes place on many different timescales. Examples include a very short-term intraday movement in which a $50 stock might climb or plunge 20¢–30¢ in a few minutes, a medium-term intraday momentum in which that stock might climb or plunge 50¢–$1.50 during the course of several hours, a short-term daily momentum in which a stock might move 5%–8% in a few days or weeks, and a longer-term daily momentum in which a stock might move 30%–40% or more during the course of many months or years.

Sometimes the momentum from the different timeframes lines up. You'll get a short-term drop during the day, within a medium-term drop, within a long-term drop. The U.S. market drop in late September and early October 2008 was filled with days when panic occurred at all timeframes. The level of uncertainty was very high, and this led to continuing panic selling and very high volatility during those weeks.

Momentum doesn't go on forever. When it slows, it generally doesn't stop; it usually reverses.

Cycles: Waxing and Waning Anxiety

Prices move in cycles. Unfortunately for traders, these are not pretty sine-wave cycles. Market price patterns don't repeat in regular form that's easy to predict. However, the market does exhibit a clear up-and-down movement. The cycles occur because of pauses and changes in momentum. Momentum runs in one direction for a while until it exhausts its fuel; then the market pauses and continues or turns the other way for a while.

Figure 4.1 depicts a chart of IBM from March 2009 through the beginning of July 2009. I have labeled the points of several short-term daily cycles in order starting with A through J. Notice that although the price of IBM moved steadily higher from late March (labeled A), the rise in prices was interspersed with declines that took place about weekly. You have a rise to A followed by a decline to B, followed by a higher rise to C and a decline to D. These cycles of rising and falling prices continued through the time of this writing. Each leg of the cycle generally lasted between three and six days.

FIGURE 4.1 Cycles

What causes these cycles? What is the impetus for the seemingly sudden change in direction?

Cycles are caused by the ebb and flow of market psychology—the waxing and waning of bullish sentiment, along with its concurrent optimism. Markets rise because market participants believe the price should be higher. The sellers are less willing to sell at the current price, and the buyers are more willing to pay a higher price. Consider the pattern in Figure 4.2.

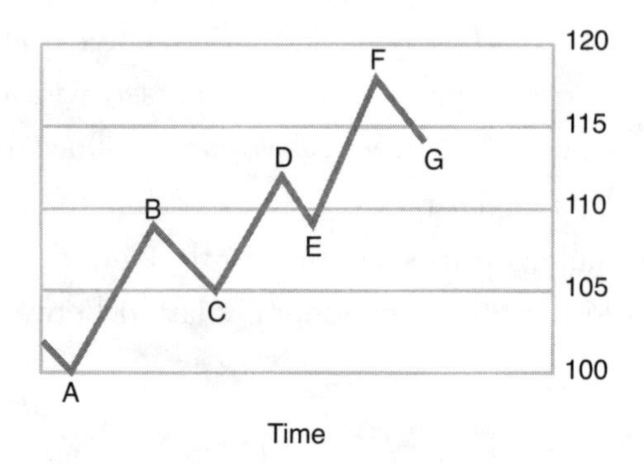

FIGURE 4.2 Cycle psychology

To understand cycles, it helps to consider what the market participants are thinking at each point in the cycle and what might be causing the changes in price direction associated with the turning points in each cycle.

Let's begin with point A. From this point, the price rises consistently from about $100 to $108 per share. Buyers are willing to pay new higher prices to complete their purchase. Sellers have been less willing to sell at lower prices, so the price has risen. At some point around $108, the buying pressure dries up because the potential buyers are no longer willing to pay higher prices. The anxious buyers who once were willing to buy at higher prices have already bought all the stock they needed. This leaves only those buyers who are more patient and willing to wait for a better opportunity, who aren't content to purchase using market orders.

At point B, sellers are now faced with a choice: Either they can wait for higher prices or, if they want to sell, they need to reduce their prices. All the anxious buyers are gone. The good times have ended for the sellers. Now they will need to use market orders to sell their stock.

Some of the potential sellers are those who bought much earlier. At any price over $105, they will be selling at a significant profit. Others potential sellers will have bought more recently, perhaps when the price was $105 or $106. They would like to sell at a profit, but they cannot do so if the price falls more than $2 or $3 off the $108 high. Other potential sellers bought at $107 or $108 and had expected the price to go much higher.

It is unlikely that those who recently bought near $108 will be the first to start selling. They bought in expectation of a profit; they will not be swayed unless the price begins to drop. It's more likely that a few of the buyers who bought at much lower prices—perhaps $80–$90—recognize an opportunity to profit from their purchases. Worrying that the trend of steadily rising prices is about to end, they look to sell. When they cannot sell at higher prices, they begin to worry that the market has reached a top. Not wanting to wait and fearing a drop, they sell at the current bid price. This behavior of selling at the market slowly drops the price.

As more traders notice the new downturn, some who bought near $105 or $106 start to worry that their profits will be gone before they get a chance to sell. Some of them begin to mildly panic and sell. Not wanting to wait, others also sell using market orders, which results in a further drop in prices.

The price drop starts a downward momentum that continues until all the nervous sellers have sold their stock. At some point just before the C label on the chart (the $105 price), the balance of power starts tipping again toward the buyers. Some buyers who have been waiting for the selling to drive prices lower start to purchase more aggressively. They start being willing to pay the higher ask price more often. The tide turns. The price starts to rise. The downward momentum is stopped.

The rising price causes other potential buyers to press their orders more aggressively. They, too, begin to worry that the price will continue to rise. They want to buy while the price is still relatively low. Because the price has recently started rising, a sense of urgency ensues. If the price continues to rise, they will lose out on potential profits.

We can model the ebb and flow between the pressure from buyers and sellers using a graph of buyer and seller anxiety. If the buyers are more anxious, the price will rise; if the sellers are more anxious, the price will decline. Figure 4.3 charts the price versus the anxiety levels of the buyers and sellers.

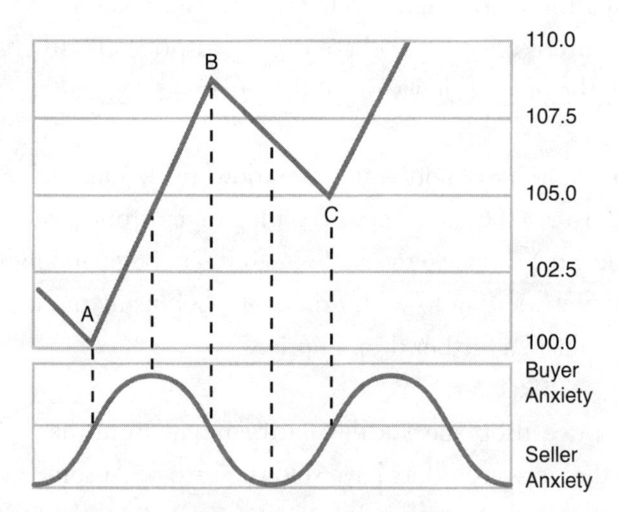

FIGURE 4.3 Buyer and seller anxiety versus price

Note how the price valleys correspond to the transition point where buyer anxiety (or desperation) begins to surpass seller anxiety (or desperation). Similarly, the price peaks represent the points where seller anxiety overtakes buyer anxiety.

The quantity of buyers versus sellers doesn't drive the price; it's the relative desperation of those buyers and sellers.

Some people think that prices go up because more buyers exist than sellers. This is not true. The number of buyers and sellers is always equal. Every trade that takes place involves one buyer and one seller. At the end of the day, the volume represents the total number of shares transacted; this is equal to the number of shares bought and the number of shares sold. The quantity of buyers versus sellers doesn't drive the price; it's the relative desperation of those buyers and sellers.

Figure 4.3 is unrealistically synchronized. Rarely are the cycles exactly the same duration. Figure 4.4 shows a more likely scenario.

Note how the cycles are no longer of uniform length. At some point between B and C on the graph, the cycle time was shortened. This means that buyer anxiety grew more suddenly than in the previous cycle.

In reality, trading cycles are not at all uniform. In the real world, both the timing of cycles and their magnitude vary. Buyer anxiety during the up leg of a cycle is rarely of the same magnitude as seller anxiety during the next down leg. Sometimes the length and duration of one direction are markedly shorter than for the other direction. In a rising market, buyer anxiety exceeds seller anxiety on average. In a declining market, seller anxiety usually exceeds buyer anxiety. These variations result in price action that has the characteristic ups and downs of market cycles.

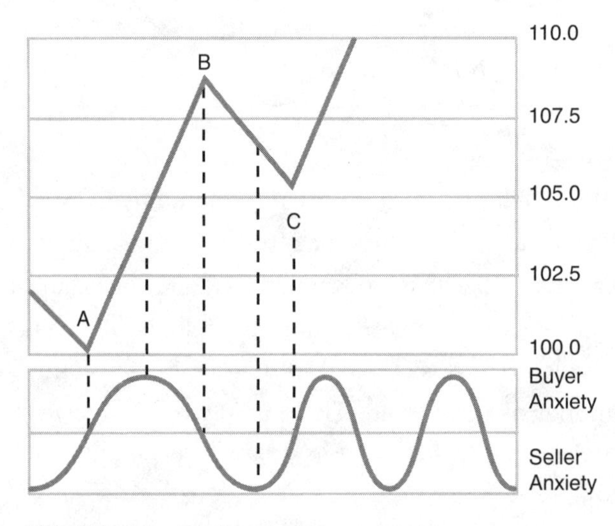

FIGURE 4.4 Cycles that are not uniform

Support and Resistance: Push Me, Pull You

Support and resistance is one of the most important concepts in market structure. Changes in cycle direction because of the crossover between buyer and seller anxiety often take place near support and resistance levels. Consider Figure 4.5.

Horizontal support and resistance always depends on an initial **anchor point**, a point on the chart that during subsequent trading days stands out as a significant visual high or low. In Figure 4.5, the point labeled A, where the price of Cisco rallied to $20 per share at the end of April, is an anchor point for the subsequent resistance. This price of $20 defines the resistance level. An anchor point takes on meaning only after at least a few days have passed and its price has not been exceeded. The point defined at A is significant because $20 is the highest trading level for several trading months.

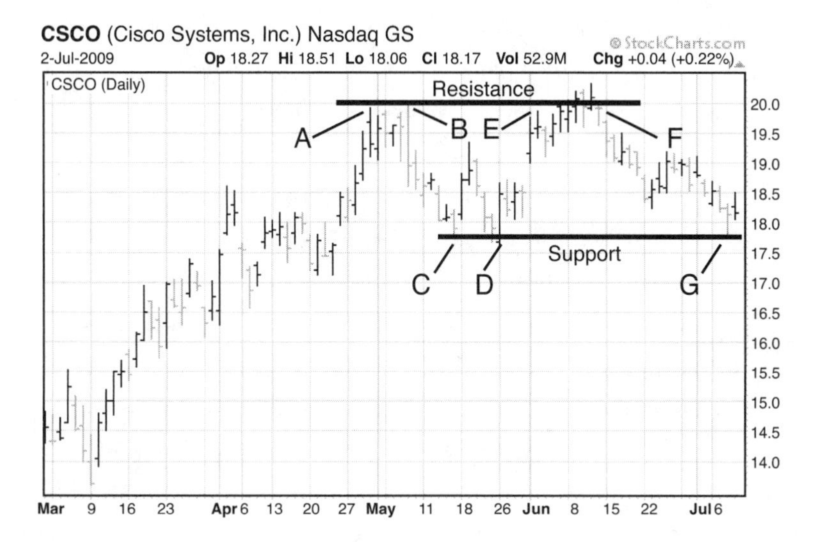

FIGURE 4.5 Support and resistance

Subsequent price points B, E, and F represent changes in cycle direction because of their proximity to the resistance level of $20 defined by the anchor point at A.

At point B, as the price nears $20 after having dropped to $19 twice, increased selling pressure will occur. Many sellers who were hoping for a better price when the market first approached $20 at A will have had their hopes tempered by the subsequent price drop. So when the price reaches that level again, they will be more anxious to sell than they were when it first hit that level. Furthermore, because the price of $20 has not been exceeded during the intervening four days, it will now seem like a high price to both buyers and sellers. Buyers will be less willing to buy at this high price and sellers will be more willing to sell.

The combination of these two factors creates a natural barrier to the price going higher—a resistance level near $20. The price is more likely to reverse course near resistance levels. Resistance levels also serve as a natural place for an up cycle to change into a down cycle. As the price nears the resistance, buyer anxiety drops and seller anxiety climbs until the sellers become more anxious to sell. They are then more willing to place market orders. This generally results in at least a temporary drop in price.

Resistance might last for only one day or for a few days. The price might not quite reach the level of resistance before it has an effect. It is not uncommon for the price to come close but not exceed the price. Consider point E. After having dropped below $18, the price rises again in late May to a high point near $19.80. At that point, it begins to falter and drops back again to near $19. The $20 price offered resistance at E even though the price did not quite reach $20.

Other times, resistance is exceeded by a small amount during several days, but the price can't seem to break out of the level defined by the resistance. Notice point F. The price exceeds $20 for a couple days but doesn't make it higher than about $20.25. It is not uncommon for resistance to have this effect. The resistance level is exceeded, but only by a little bit. Buyers *are not* anxious enough to drive the price higher, and sellers *are* anxious that they will not see this price again, so they panic first.

Now consider support. At point C on the chart, the price has established a low at $17.80. Subsequent to this point, the price rises to a level of about $19.35 and then descends again to just below the price at point C, at about $17.75, where it finds support. Buyers become more anxious than sellers at this point. They consider $17.75–$17.80 to be a low price, and they are more willing to place market orders, so the price rises. Other potential buyers don't want to miss out on the low prices, so they join them. This causes the price to rise further.

A very significant part of the reason prices appear to "bounce" off support and resistance levels is that many traders have observed this effect and expect to see it in the future. Therefore, support and resistance is partly a self-fulfilling prophecy. Traders buy at support levels in expectation of the rise in prices due to the support itself. Traders sell at resistance levels in expectation of the decline in prices due to the resistance itself. When multiplied, these effects make support and resistance one of the most powerful concepts in trading. The behavior of market participants reinforces the effects themselves.

Finally, notice the effect of the same support level almost two months later when the price hits $17.85 after having climbed to more than $20 in the intervening period. Once again, a bounce occurs at G, where the price climbs to $18.85. This sort of bounce is very common. Even if the price goes down during the subsequent day or two, a temporary bounce at support and resistance levels is one of the most reliable concepts in trading.

Euphoria and Despair: The Thrill of Victory and the Agony of Defeat

Another reliable concept in trading is the overextension that occurs at the end of rapid price moves. Sometimes these moves take place during months or weeks, but sometimes they take place during a few days.

In many ways, we can liken these moves to what might happen to a small weight attached to the end of a fishing pole. If you move the pole slowly, the weight will move with the pole. If you move the pole swiftly, the weight will move but a lag will occur because of the weight's inertia. The weighted end will move in the direction of the pole's movement, but the end of the pole will overshoot and spring back toward the original position. Having overshot again, it will move back toward the pole's new position. With each successive cycle, the amount the weight overshoots will decrease until finally the weighted end of the pole comes to rest at equilibrium in the pole's new position. If you plotted the end of the pole's position after you moved it suddenly lower, you might get a graph that looks similar to Figure 4.6.

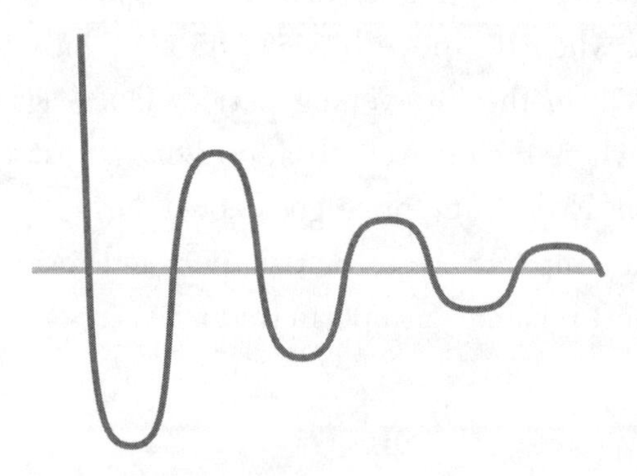

FIGURE 4.6 Damped harmonic oscillator

In physics, this type of movement is associated with a **damped harmonic oscillator**, a series of progressively smaller waves that oscillate about a center line. A plucked guitar or piano string behaves similar to a damped harmonic oscillator; the vibrations are larger at first, and then the oscillations die down over time.

Markets often act similar to damped harmonic oscillators. As with the weighted end of a fishing pole, they often overshoot when they move and then bounce around slowly to find a new equilibrium after a large price displacement. Consider the graph in Figure 4.7 of the price for auto parts supplier Dana Holdings.

FIGURE 4.7 Dana Holdings price displacements

Note how the price oscillates around the $2 level after the initial rapid price displacement. The price climbs more than 150% in two days. On the third day, it opens and climbs to $2.75 and then drops more than half its value while setting a low of $1.35 before finally closing at $1.70. The following day, it continues to oscillate around

$2, with a low of $1.65 and a high of $2.50. The second day's range of 85¢ is considerably lower than the first day after the large displacement's range of $1.40. The oscillation continues the following day, but the range is reduced even further to about 40¢.

The price descends for a few days and then begins to oscillate around a new lower equilibrium point of $1.50. These oscillations also continue for a few days.

The initial displacement resulted in substantial oscillation and the subsequent displacement also produced substantial oscillation. A sizeable price movement almost always causes a large increase in volatility as the price tries to find a new equilibrium point.

The one major exception to this rule is that price movements can displace and then very quickly return to the old price level. This tends to act similar to our fishing pole with the weight on the end if we moved it up sharply and then just as sharply moved it back down to its original position. It would create a large overshooting on the upside, followed by an oscillation of high volatility around the new equilibrium point. Consider the chart for Dry Ships, Inc. (DRYS), in Figure 4.8.

Note that the price move from early April, when the price of DRYS was around $5, to its peak of over $11 just a few weeks later in early May represented an increase of more than 120%. No doubt many of the anxious buyers who were willing to pay higher prices during the run-up from $5 to over $11 were thinking of the price just a few months earlier, when DRYS traded over $17. Others might have been thinking of the highs of the previous May, when DRYS traded over $110. Compared to these prices, a run-up to $11 must have appeared small.

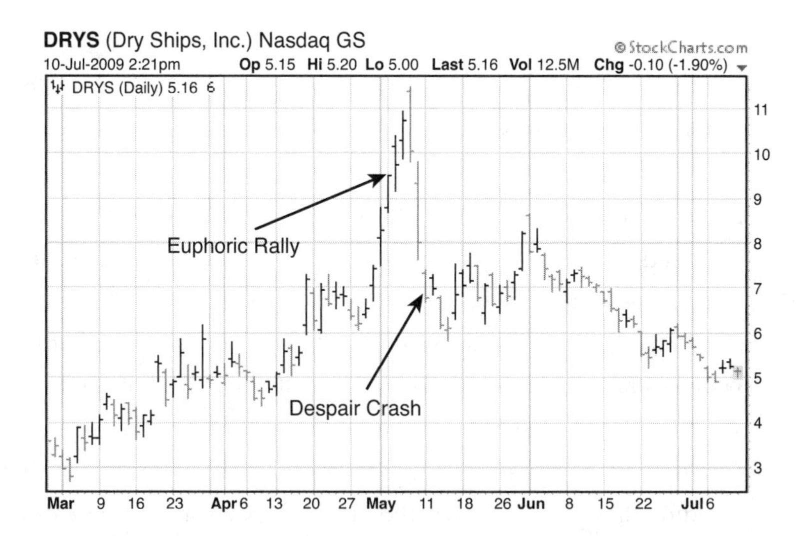

FIGURE 4.8 Price displacement and return to equilibrium

However, the market thought otherwise. Similar to the end of the fishing pole, as quick as the price ran up, it quickly snapped back and oscillated around the new equilibrium point of $7 per share for the next few weeks.

The DRYS chart in Figure 4.8 illustrates two important concepts: a euphoric rally followed by a despair crash. An exhaustion rally takes place at the end of a period of steady price increase. In this case, the price had risen for more than two months from about $3.50 to $6 to $7 in late April. After that point, it rose dramatically, gaining 50% in just five days. This was the exhaustion rally. At this stage, emotion takes over and buyers are paying whatever price they need to get the stock. The master traders might have bought during the first day or two of the run-up, but they were not buying toward the end, as the price continued an unsustainable vertical climb.

Vertical climbs will always end.

Vertical climbs will always end. You can make a lot of money during the climb if you got in early. Buying late during a vertical climb is a recipe for disaster.

The psychological power of the buyers quickly dried up as the price opened up over $11 and then dropped below $10 on the same day, beginning a six-day descent to $6 by mid-May. Market sentiment can change this quickly. One day it might be irrationally bullish. The very next day, it might be irrationally bearish. During these times, traders can potentially make (and lose) a lot of money. The difference between the master traders and the others is that master traders know how to recognize the signs of exhaustion, overextension, and panic—novices don't.

But how do the basics of market structure interconnect to present opportunities for making money—the elusive edge in trading? How does intuition fit in with this market structure? How do we use our gut instinct to identify the opportunities that present themselves?

These are good questions that we'll answer soon enough. First, we need to examine the proper role of intuition and instinct, and how this differs from rational analysis. We need to provide a firm basis for trusting your gut.

CHAPTER 5

Training and Trusting Your Gut

"Intuition is reason in a hurry."

—Holbrook Jackson

The Monaco Grand Prix is one of the most famous races in the world and one of the most well-known sporting events in general. The Grand Prix's track is set in the narrow, winding streets of Monte Carlo, where trackside spectators can watch cars speeding by much closer than in a typical race. The track is also one of the toughest in racing; the 77-lap circuit allows no margin for error. For this reason, the best drivers usually win the Monaco Grand Prix. It is a racer's race.

The track in Monaco has one very interesting feature: A significant portion of it is an underground tunnel. It can be tricky for drivers to adjust their eyes from the light of day to darkness and then back to bright daylight again. When drivers emerge from the tunnel, they have compromised vision through the fastest portion of the track.

The Argentine racer Juan Manuel Fangio, known as "El Maestro" (Spanish for "The Master"), is regarded by many as the best race car driver of all time. His five Formula One championships held the record for 46 years. His first Formula One victory occurred at the 1950 Monaco Grand Prix.

Fangio started the 1950 Monaco Grand Prix in the pole position, and he held the lead after the first lap. As he emerged from the tunnel into daylight, Fangio braked suddenly instead of maintaining his speed into the straightaway and raised his hand to warn other drivers. In doing so, he avoided a pileup around the blind corner obscured by the balustrade on the side of the track.

On the first lap behind him, Nino Farina had skidded out because a section of the track—after the chicane (small S-curve) and before the corner known as the Tobacconist's corner—was wet from blowing sea spray. Eight separate cars crashed into the pileup. That meant that half the lineup—9 of the 18 cars—was involved in this one crash. Fortunately, no one was seriously injured.

Why had Fangio braked? "I could detect agitation among the spectators," he recalled. "They were not looking at me leading the race, but were looking the other way." As Fangio noted, they normally would be facing the lead car in the race, alerted to his presence by the deep resonating rumble as he came out of the tunnel. However, instead of seeing the crowd's faces this time—which would make the spectators a relatively light-colored blur as he passed by at high speed—he was seeing a darker blur from the backs of their heads as they turned away to look at the crash. Out of the corner of his eye, this triggered something in his subconscious, right-brain thinking.

At the speeds of a Formula One race, even in 1950, drivers had no time for deliberative, conscious decision making. El Maestro's intuition and quick reaction saved the race—and possibly his life.

Emotion Versus Intuition

One misconception people have about right-brain-dominant people is that they use emotion as the basis for their decision making. They think that somehow these people are relying on a more primitive and, therefore, inferior process for making decisions. This bias against right-brain-dominant thinking comes from the mistaken belief that right-brain thinking is based on emotions and is therefore somehow less rational than left-brain thinking.

Intuition is profoundly logical; it's just logic of a different sort that is communicated via body sensation and feeling instead of conscious rationale.

Juan Fangio didn't have a bias against his intuition; he knew to trust it. If you want to be a master trader, you need to learn to trust your intuition, too. In this chapter, I show how intuition is not magical, but simply uses a different mechanism for arriving at its answers. George Soros's back pain might appear supernatural, but it is not—it's simply his body's way of communicating intuition. This intuition is profoundly logical; it's just logic of a different sort that is communicated via body sensation and feeling instead of conscious rationale.

Distinguishing between emotional feelings and intuition that comes from the right brain is often difficult. In English, the word *feeling* is used to describe both concepts: intuitive responses for which no conscious logical basis exists, and the more primitive, purely emotional responses. One reason is that both feelings and intuition make their presence known through the same part of the brain. Often the output of the logical process of the right brain comes to our conscious thought through the emotional center of the brain, the limbic system.

American physician and neuroscientist Paul MacLean first proposed the idea that the human brain is a triune brain, meaning that it is divided into three separate sections. He called the first section the **R-Complex**, also sometimes called the **reptilian brain**. It consists of the brain stem and cerebellum. The reptilian brain controls muscles, balance, and autonomic functions such as breathing and heartbeats. It is responsible for instinctive survival behaviors and reacts directly to certain stimuli.

MacLean called the second section the **limbic system**, also sometimes called the **paleo-mammalian** brain (Latin for "ancient mammal brain"). This section consists of a large number of smaller organs that are situated around the brain stem, including the **amygdala**, the **hypothalamus**, and the **hippocampus**. The limbic system is responsible for emotion and feelings.

Considerable evidence also suggests that the limbic system is at the center of the brain's evaluation systems. Emotion and feelings are, after all, evaluations of value. Animals, including humans, have pleasurable or pleasant feelings toward those things that benefit them. Animals have negative sensations or feelings toward those things that might harm them. Sweet, healthy food tastes good. Food that contains natural poisons generally tastes bad. The sense of taste provides a natural mechanism for evaluating between food choices.

The limbic system's evaluation mechanisms manifest in other ways. For example, damage to the hippocampus results in the inability to store memories. Scientists theorize that this occurs because of the inability to sort out which inputs are worthy of remembering. If the brain can't rate memories, it can't store new ones.

The third section is the **neocortex** (Latin for "new bark"), or **neomammalian** brain (Latin for "new mammal brain"). This section is present only in mammals. The neocortex is a thin layer—composed of six individual layers of neuron cells—that surrounds the rest of the brain. In many smaller mammals, the neocortex is smooth. However, in larger mammals, primates, and humans, the neocortex takes on a wrinkled shape that enables it to have a much larger surface area for a given brain size. The neocortex appears to have the same basic composition in all sections of the brain.

Compared with other animals, human beings have an oversized brain. The human brain is much larger as a percentage of body mass than the brain of any other animal. Most of this extra mass is contained in the neocortex. The neocortex is the part of the brain that is responsible for higher-order thinking. It contains most of what makes us smarter than other animals.

Because the neocortex is the source of human intelligence, it is important to note that both the left and right hemispheres are parts of the same neocortex. Both hemispheres are intelligent and logical at their core.

Top or Bottom?

Nevertheless, it can be easy to confuse the feelings that have an emotional basis with the feelings that have a thinking basis when the right hemisphere performs that thinking. The major reason for this is that the thinking of the left hemisphere is top down and linear, but the thinking of the right hemisphere is bottom up and parallel.

Top-down thinking requires a conscious connection between thoughts, a direction of attention from one connected idea to another. It proceeds in an orderly, linear manner and connects smaller parts in an intentional logical tree. Our attention directs this process so that our thoughts are controlled and proceed in what we think of as a "logical" progression.

Bottom-up thinking...only appears to be magical because the conclusions of the right brain come to us fully formed and seemingly without supporting evidence.

Bottom-up thinking does not require a conscious connection of thought—in fact, it does not require any of our attention. Therefore, bottom-up thinking can often appear to be a magical or psychic phenomenon, but it is not. It is as rational as linear top-down thinking. It only *appears* to be magical because the conclusions of the right brain come to us fully formed and seemingly without supporting evidence. However, the evidence is there. It just remains hidden because of the different way in which the right brain processes information—in a bottom-up approach instead of the top-down approach of the left brain.

During the last several decades, scientists have used new technologies to examine the cells of the neocortex, which has helped them understand the brain's function. They have determined which areas are used for higher thinking and which areas are used for visual and auditory processing; they have mapped virtually the entire brain by function. One surprising result has emerged from this research: The brain's various functional areas exhibit very little difference in the neocortex structure. If you examined a small section of the right hemisphere, you would not easily be able to determine where it came from or which hemisphere it was. All but the experts would have trouble pinpointing exactly where a particular section fit into the larger neocortex.

This means that no structural difference exists between the left and right hemispheres. Neuroscientists have found that, in the entire neocortex, the six layers of neurons appear to be interconnected in the same ways, regardless of which area of the brain they examine. Therefore, the logical process the left and right hemispheres use must be more similar than different.

Both hemispheres, and neural networks in general, find patterns and classify information. The difference is the order and reason for the classification. Consider two different leisure activities: assembling a large Lego set into a race car and assembling a large, complex jigsaw puzzle.

In assembling the Lego set, the process is generally **top down**. First, you look at the available pieces to determine the general complexity of the car that you might build from them. Then you determine, based on colors and shapes, which pieces might be appropriate for the various parts of the car. Then you might try to assemble the more difficult parts of the car first—perhaps the wheels or main part of the body and then the fairings and decorative parts later. At each step in the process, you would know what part you were building and why you were working on that part. As you assembled the parts, the race car would take form in clearly delineated stages. This is an example of a top-down process and top-down thinking.

Contrast this with the **bottom-up** way that you assemble a jigsaw puzzle. With a jigsaw puzzle, the most important aspect of the problem is *determining which pieces fit together.* First, you broadly categorize the pieces. Then you separate them into different colors and shapes. You find the corners and edges, and then you begin to search for the edge pieces that might fit with a particular corner, based on the shape of the edges and the color shade. After finding the pieces that fit with a particular corner, you continue to search for new pieces that match up with the pieces that you just placed next to the corners, continuing this process until you cannot easily find a match. Then you start the same process again at the other corners until you have built the entire frame for the puzzle.

After building the frame, you work on the easiest remaining section. In most puzzles, you know what picture you are assembling, so you can determine what might be easy to assemble based on the drawing itself. Perhaps it is some lines in the picture, or a particular color shade that appears in only a small section. Some puzzle builders prefer not to look at the picture on the box as they are building because they like the challenge of a harder task. These advanced builders are the ultimate in bottom-up puzzle assemblers.

With each section, you reach a point at which finding the pieces that fit becomes more difficult. Generally, this occurs when the shape and color of the piece you are looking for is very common. When you reach such a point, you generally move on to another section of the puzzle, looking again for relatively easy pieces to fit. As the puzzle building proceeds, fewer unmatched pieces remain, making it easier to find pieces that fit a particular spot. That is why *the pace of assembling the puzzle is fast at first,* then slows down as you work on the more difficult sections, and then *speeds up with a final acceleration at the end* when all the pieces quickly come together into one whole picture.

The important contrast between assembling the Lego race car and building a jigsaw puzzle is that, with the Lego race car, you concentrate on *how each piece fits into your overall whole* and whether the parts fit the higher vision. As you proceed, you are consciously aware of what part you are working on and how it fits into the whole.

With the bottom-up approach of building the jigsaw puzzle, what matters during the process of assembly is not how each piece fits into the larger picture you are building, but *how each piece connects to the other pieces* and *the potential connections that each piece might have.* With the Lego race car, you start with the vision of the car in your head. With the jigsaw puzzle, you start by assembling the pieces that seem to go together most obviously.

The bottom-up thoughts of the right brain sometimes comes together in a quick snap, such as during the last stages of a jigsaw puzzle when the pieces all come together. This snap often seems like a feeling or intuition that comes out of nowhere because our left brain is not able to understand how the pieces were assembled in the bottom-up process.

Intuition and Time Pressure

I believe that most left-brain-dominant people have great difficulty trusting their intuition. In these individuals, the left brain is in charge and wants explanations. When the right brain can supply them, the left brain is satisfied. In contrast, if the intuition comes as a feeling, a vibe, or a bodily sensation, left-brain-dominant people have a hard time giving the intuition any credence. The left brain wants explanations; if you can't supply them, it won't believe an intuition. This lack of trust in your intuition can be a big impediment to your ability to improve in your trading.

Even for the most highly left-brain-dominant people, however, there are times when the right brain takes over. According to Professor Gerard Hodgkinson of the Centre for Organisational Strategy, Learning, and Change at Leeds University Business School, "People usually experience true intuition when they are under severe time pressure or in a situation of information overload or acute danger, where conscious analysis of the situation may be difficult or impossible."

In the case of another Formula One driver who experienced an intuition to brake, bearing an uncanny similarity to Fangio's, Professor Hodgkinson explains:

> The driver couldn't explain why he felt he should stop, but the urge was much stronger than his desire to win the race. The driver underwent forensic analysis by psychologists afterwards, where he was shown a video to mentally relive the event. In hindsight, he realized that the crowd, which would have normally been cheering him on, wasn't looking at him coming up to the bend but was looking the other way in a static, frozen way. That was the cue. He didn't consciously process this, but he knew something was wrong and stopped in time.

Interestingly, although the urge was strong enough to get him to brake sharply, this driver, like Fangio, was not conscious of the thought process that provided the urge to brake. Even though the impulse to stop was initiated by a bottom-up notice from the right brain, the interaction with the conscious left-brain thought process came through what the driver felt as an urge. It did not come to him through a conscious process in which he noticed the crowd; thought to himself, "How strange that they are turned away and not looking in this direction"; and then thought, "There must have been an accident." That would have taken far too much time.

Instead, what happened is that the right brain noticed the danger sign all at once and, bypassing the left brain, sent a signal directly to his limbic system, where it became an urge—a strong feeling—that then triggered his sudden and strong braking by directly interacting with the part of his brain that pushed his foot down on the brake. He had no time to walk the left brain through the logical steps required before taking action. The body needed to act now, and the right brain had enough information to force an override of the normal process. So it did. Only in retrospect could the driver determine what his right brain had noticed.

Had the driver been new to racing, or had this been his first major race, his right brain likely would not have had enough information with which to compare the behavior of the crowd. Therefore, he would not have noticed the unusual way in which they were looking down the track. His lack of experience would likely have contributed to a serious accident.

This is one of the reasons traders need to train their intuition. If you do not have enough raw experience or you have not supplied your right brain with enough trading examples, you will not be able to accurately and swiftly recognize the patterns that a more experienced trader will see with ease. You will be more likely to encounter problems without any warning from your right brain's intuition. You will be more likely to miss opportunities that an experienced trader will notice without thinking.

Intuition comes into play when conscious analysis of the information is impossible because of too much information or too little time.

Remember that Professor Hodgkinson noted that people experience true intuition where conscious analysis of the situation might be difficult or impossible. When you are under severe time pressure, you don't have time to make a conscious analysis. When too much information exists, making a conscious analysis of all the information is impossible. So intuition comes into play when conscious analysis of the information is impossible because of too much information or too little time.

Sometimes the markets become so hectic that you won't have much time to make trading decisions. During a crash or after a big unexpected market event, you might not have time for a full analysis of what to do and why. During these times, if you have trained your gut, you will be able to trust it. You will be able to rely on your intuition to save you from impending danger.

In the case of the drivers' sudden braking, the series of events was initiated by the right brain noticing that something wasn't right. Because the drivers didn't have enough time to consciously analyze what was going on, the right brain induced a quick reaction by bypassing the left brain's conscious thinking. It went directly for the seat of emotion in the limbic system, sending a strong "feeling" that something was not right and that immediate braking was the best option.

Limbic Ranking and Preferences

The kind of signal you get from a properly trained right brain often comes that way—as a feeling. The limbic system is responsible for these feelings, which are part of its evaluation and preference mechanism. What course or option do you prefer? What kind of food do you want to eat? What color pleases you? What smells bring good thoughts? This same preference and ranking system is often used to rank your preferences based on right-brain thinking that takes place outside of conscious thought.

Sometimes you are inexplicably drawn to something or someone. Or you might find that you have a strong aversion to some object, smell, or person without any conscious explanation. You might say that you got "bad vibes" or "good vibes" from someone or a particular place. Other times, the work of the right brain connects directly to your conscious thought. It generally does this by bringing your attention to some thought or item that your senses have just seen or heard. The right brain performs this activity very well. It observes and notices. Bottom-up thinking often produces observations—fully assembled pieces of thought characterized by causative or associative connections between various phenomena.

You might notice that a particular phenomenon tends to precede another phenomenon. For example, you might notice that budding of the trees tends to precede the coming of the spring rains. You might notice that a certain coworker tends to come into work late on Friday mornings and that the weekly poker game at his apartment is on Thursday nights. You notice a potential causal connection between the two phenomena.

When trading, you might observe something and note to yourself, "That's odd. It seems like when there is a vertical run-up in a stock, there is often a gap down right near the top." These conscious observations are easy to handle. They interface with our linear left-brain thinking quite seamlessly.

The feelings you get from intuition outside our consciousness are more difficult to handle for left-brain-dominant people who always seek an explanation for their actions and thoughts. They often need to be able to connect the dots between conscious thoughts to make a decision.

Contrast this with the way the very best athletes use their intuition and subconscious to move without making conscious decisions. Sports legends at the top of their game often talk about moments of "flow" or times when they're "in the zone." On these occasions, time seems to slow down and their play seems effortless. Talented players who find moments of flow often have practiced for years, so their motor skills centers and their nervous systems already know how to do what needs to be done to perform well.

Invariably, conscious decision making gets in the way of peak performance.

Invariably, conscious decision making gets in the way of peak performance. However, the skills gained through years of training can come out if athletes are willing to release control of their bodies to their right brains. When an athlete has trained hard and has played often enough, the right brain already knows what to do. Conscious decision making isn't necessary; it only slows things down.

Juan Fangio relinquished his driving to his instincts while racing. Besides the 1950 Monaco Grand Prix, Fabio famously avoided crashes in three other races. In two of them, he went on to win the race. He was able to deduce the other drivers' intent and skill level through tiny movements of their vehicles. He knew when they were getting into trouble before they did. This helped him avoid other accidents because he could anticipate them and react quickly to them without thinking.

In the 1953 Italian Grand Prix at Monza, Alberto Ascari and Nino "Dr. Giuseppe" Farina were leading Fangio on the last lap. They both tried to pass another driver and were forced off their line during that attempt. They both crashed as a result, and Fangio, following directly behind them, was able to miss them to take the lead and victory.

The 1955 Le Mans race was a famous tragedy. Lance Macklin's Austin Healy swerved to avoid a Jaguar that was stopping for a pit stop. The Jaguar—with the new disk brakes—stopped much more quickly than the Austin Healy, which had only the older drum brakes. Pierre Levegh crashed his Mercedes from behind into Macklin's decelerating Austin Healy. His car disintegrated and flew into the crowd, killing 80 people. Fangio was following close behind Levegh and was able to avoid the Jaguar and the crash, to continue to safety.

On the second lap of the 1957 Monaco Grand Prix, Stirling Moss crashed into a barrier while holding the lead. Mike Hawthorn, Peter Collins, and Fangio were following close behind. Hawthorn and Collins piled up one after the other, but Fangio managed to steer clear of all three cars that crashed ahead of him. Once again, Fangio went on to win the race and, eventually, the overall Formula One championship for the year.

Some people might think that Fangio's uncanny ability to avoid crashes was the result of superior reflexes, but Fangio was much older than the typical driver. He hadn't started driving Formula One until he was 38 years old. He was 45 in the 1957 Monaco Grand Prix. Fangio didn't have superior reflexes; he had superior instinct and intuition.

These same principles apply to world-class trading. Master traders train and study to educate their right brains so they, too, can have superior instinct and intuition. Because they have an experienced sense of intuition, they know they can trust their gut. This gives them a decided edge when danger comes, or when market opportunities arise that require decisive action.

In upcoming chapters, I show how you can develop your gut instinct and improve your trading through proper training so that you, too, can become a master trader.

CHAPTER 6

Trading Smarts

"Intuition and concepts constitute…the elements of all our knowledge, so that neither concepts without an intuition in some way corresponding to them, nor intuition without concepts, can yield knowledge."

—Immanuel Kant

When I started trading, Richard Dennis trained me in methods he had carefully researched. Then he gave me a $2 million trading account to manage after only a month of trading a smaller practice account. I was lucky.

Most of you reading this book won't be so lucky. You'll have to develop your own techniques.

Don't leave your left brain behind in this process. If you want to trade with both your intuition and your intellect, you need to pick trading strategies that work for your whole mind. Systematic intellectual traders who ignore their intuition are losing out on great potential benefit. So are discretionary traders who attempt to bypass or override their intellect—those who neglect to provide a firm rational basis for their trades.

Every trading method should be grounded in a firm intellectual framework.

Every trading method should be grounded in a firm intellectual framework. In this chapter, I show the basis for a specific method that I use as an example in the next several chapters. I like to start with the basics, such as the rationale for the method, and build my strategies from there. The first step in building a rationale is choosing a type of trading method that works for you.

Step by Step

When I resumed trading in 2001, I started an online trading discussion forum. Traders, and those who wanted to become traders, could post questions to more experienced traders. Many questions were directed to me. Some were specific questions about the methods we used as Turtles, which were easy to answer. Traders who wanted to emulate our success asked the more difficult questions. They wanted to be long-term trend followers.

I had to tell them the truth: For most people, long-term trend following is not a viable way to trade because

- Most people don't have the necessary amount of money to have a reasonable chance of earning good profits.
- You can't earn the 100% average annual returns I earned as a Turtle using the same methods we once used.
- Trading using a long-term trend-following approach requires the ability to stomach sizeable drawdowns, which most people don't have the emotional constitution for.

Trying to trade with a system that you can't get behind with your whole mind is pointless. You need to find a method that harmonizes with your whole mind and your psychological makeup. For most people, the old Turtle-style method is not that system.

So if trend following isn't suitable for most people, what sort of trading is?

Is it swing trading, in which the trades last for days or a few weeks; or day trading, in which the trades last for minutes or hours? Fortunately, most traders can easily make this decision because the process of elimination leaves them with only one viable choice. For most traders, swing trading is the obvious choice.

Day trading requires that you devote the entire day to trading. This is not an ideal scenario for many traders who maintain a full-time job and trade a small account on the side. Most traders need an approach that won't take up all their time—one that they can do part-time while supporting themselves with another job until they have honed their trading skills and built their trading account to the level required to earn a living from trading itself.

Day trading also requires quick judgment and decision-making skills. Many traders don't possess these skills. Active traders have a hard time reacting quickly enough to make money while competing against professional day traders that have generally been trading 24/7 for years, if not decades. Some people like the speed of day trading. I don't. From my personal perspective, it requires too much attention during the day and doesn't leave me much time for other interests.

For these reasons, swing trading is the most viable option for most traders. You can trade with a smaller account, it won't consume all your time, and it doesn't require lightning-quick reaction. Swing trading also fits my personal lifestyle better. You can pick up trading for a while and then stop while you are doing something else. Because the trades normally last only a few days, you can start and stop more easily. During the day, you usually just need to wait for market alerts to fire, so you can be doing something else. I have many other interests, so this style suits me well.

Swing trading is also a type of trading that benefits from a whole-brain trading style. If you use your intuition, you will be able to find many more opportunities than you would if you use only one part of your mind. Swing trading benefits from both intellect and intuition.

The Source of Opportunity

If you want to be one of the few who reliably and consistently make money from the market, you need to find a strategy that gives you an advantage, an edge. To build such a strategy, you combine the building-block basics we learned in Chapter 4, "The Structure of the Markets," in particular ways to extract profits.In this chapter, I put those building blocks together in a strategy that enables the left brain and right brain to do what they do best.

My rationale for this trading approach draws from the basics. First, recall that human psychology is the foundation upon which all successful trading is built. Markets are made up of large numbers of interacting *Homo sapiens,* each with their own individual agenda. Even when they use computer networks and programs to execute their trades, somewhere behind the scenes for every trade is an individual trader who directed the computer to execute that trade using a specific set of algorithms. To beat the markets, you first need to understand these traders' motivations, the impetus behind the direction and timing of the trades. Then you need to find times when the markets participants in aggregate have mispriced the market—when the market does not reflect the "right" price.

Many people, especially economists, are fond of saying that markets always reflect the "correct" price. This is one of the conclusions of the efficient-market hypothesis: Markets already reflect all known information, so they quickly respond to new information. Therefore, these economists believe that it is impossible to consistently win money by trading the market because the market already reflects all known information. They attribute any success by traders to mere random chance—the lucky monkey theorem.

Master traders know that *Homo sapiens* are not completely rational. We have emotions, are sometimes afraid, are sometimes overconfident, and display cognitive biases. For these reasons, we sometimes overreact or underreact. Therefore, the price is not always "right."

The way to reliably make money from the markets is to identify repeatable psychological market phenomena in which market prices appear to *already reflect* an overreaction or underreaction on the part of market participants, and *trade against that reaction* or *anticipate* an overreaction or underreaction based on previous market behavior. You can make money from both overreactions and underreactions, either by predicting them or by reacting to them. Predicting market prices themselves is very hard. Predicting human reaction to market prices is somewhat easier. But easiest of all is *detecting what has already happened* and *reacting to that existing market condition.*

If the market overreacts, you can make money by anticipating a return to "correct" price levels. If the market underreacts, you can also make money by anticipating a return to "correct" price levels. In each of these respective scenarios, the meaning of "correct" is different. In the case of an underreaction of a price toward the upside, the "correct" price level is above the market price, so you can profit by buying at the market price and anticipating an eventual return to the "correct" price. In the case of an overreaction of a price toward the upside, the "correct" price level is below the market price, so you can profit by selling at the market price and anticipating an eventual return to the "correct" price.

Markets as Emergent Systems

For example, the market reactions for most stocks are aggregations of the behavior of thousands of individual traders and investors. The aggregation of these behaviors often exhibits a repeatable consistency that is not readily apparent if one examines the behavior of the individuals independently. This emergence of more complex behavior out of the behavior of interacting individuals is found in nature and has been studied as a phenomenon known as **emergent systems**.

Two common examples of a behavior stemming from an emergent system are schooling in fish and flocking in birds. In both of these examples, large groups of individuals coordinate their movements with the group so that an entire school of fish or flock of birds appears to be guided by a common thought. Scientists who study emergent systems have used simple computer algorithms to model similar behaviors, showing that simple rules among individuals often suffice to specify seemingly complex behavior at the group level.

In simulations, a group of fish that simply point themselves in the direction that is the average of the fish nearest to them will very closely mimic the behavior of a large school of fish. By orienting themselves parallel to the average direction that their closest peers point to, fish can school. This is a classic example of **emergent behavior**, and the composite school of fish is a classic example of an **emergent system**.

The repeatable nature of the emergent behavior in markets is the very source of the potential for profit.

The emergent behavior associated with markets develops in much the same way. When considered in isolation, each individual trader and investor exhibits relatively simple and easy-to-understand behavior, but the market seems to behave as if it were a separate entity. The repeatable nature of the emergent behavior in markets is the very source of the potential for profit. For this reason, learning to trade the markets effectively requires understanding emergent behavior and the forces that drive such behavior.

Chapter 4 covered the most important emergent behavior: cycles, market inertia and momentum, and euphoria and despair. You can make money using just knowledge of these basics.

One strategy that uses these components to illustrate the proper way to utilize left-brain smarts and right-brain intuition is the **rebound swing method**. But before we get into the specifics of that method, I want to describe the important components to any swing-trading strategy.

Swing-Trading Setups

The key to swing trading is identifying changes in the daily price-chart cycles—the transitions between periods when buyer anxiety dominates and periods when seller anxiety dominates. The changes in cycle by themselves are not enough to make a great trade because not every cycle presents a good trade opportunity.

One of the most common mistakes I have seen among traders is the tendency to want to take every trade possible.

One of the most common mistakes I have seen among traders is the tendency to want to take every trade possible. Some traders think that if they make a lot of trades, they will make a lot of money. They believe that more trades equals more money.

The problem with this approach is that all trades are not created equal. Not all market environments are suitable for every trading style. You need to have patience and recognize when the market is right for your trading abilities. The period just after a huge market crash might not be a good time to trade. Sometimes sitting on the sidelines and waiting for the volatility to subside a little is better. Sometimes you need to wait for the volatility to return.

Good swing trading is similar to surfing at the beach. Surfers let most of the waves pass them by. They wait for the big waves that are set up correctly. Then they time the drop-in just right so they catch the wave as it is forming. If they go too early, the wave will crash over the top of them. If they go too late, the wave will pass them by without carrying them forward. In the same way, not every potential market cycle should be traded, just as not every wave should be attacked. When I build a swing-trading method, I am looking for a way of identifying the best market waves and of timing the drop-in.

There's no sure thing, but when the overall market is right, the odds for certain trades will tip in your favor. This is the time to take trades. Master traders learn to develop criteria to determine exactly when the odds tip in the trader's favor, including these:

- **Market environment**—Does the stock market need to be trending up, sideways, or down? Should it be volatile or quiet?

- **Setup**—Conditions that indicate a trade is ready to be taken. These are often combinations of several short- and medium-term factors.
- **Triggering event**—Specific event that indicates a trade should be taken.
- **Exit event**—Specific event that indicates a trade should be exited.

Now let's look at the specific criteria for the rebound swing method.

The Rebound Swing Method

If you want your intellect to buy into a trading method, you need to build that method on a sound premise. Your intellect wants you to build your trading strategies on intellectually sound principles. If you can't articulate these principles consciously and apart from your intuition, you will be leaving your intellect behind when you make decisions. Without the buy-in of your left brain, you won't be as confident in your decisions. You want to use both intuition and smarts in your trading.

The premise of the rebound swing method is that the market generally moves several days in one direction after a rebound off of clear support and resistance. Therefore, this particular swing-trading method is particularly well suited to range-bound markets. It is also suited for trading in the direction of the major trend during major bull- or bear-market moves.

Whole-mind trading should begin with a clear vision of the model of the ideal version of a trade. The left brain's job is to develop the idealized models—the idealized vision of what a "perfect" trade looks like. Then the right brain's job is to find examples that most closely fit the ideal vision. To give you some idea of how this works, I begin with a model for the rebound swing method, and then I show one specific example that comes close to that ideal. I then discuss the reasons that the specific model doesn't fit that ideal, as well as the reasons those differences don't matter.

Figure 6.1 shows a model for the ideal rebound swing trade.

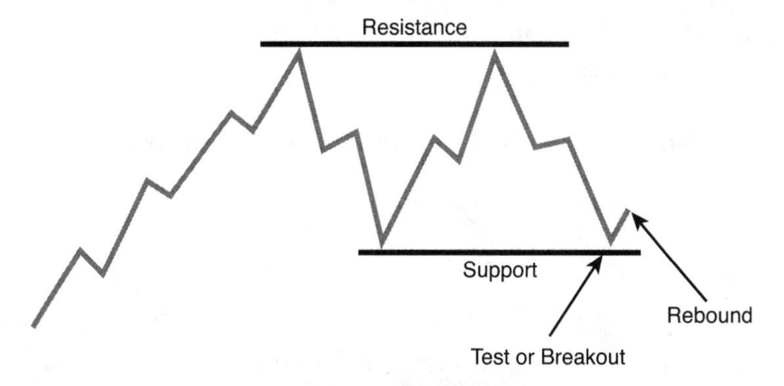

FIGURE 6.1 The ideal rebound swing trade

This model illustrates a rebound swing buy trade made in an up market. The basic idea is to buy at the beginning of a rebound off a support level when the distance from the support to the resistance is significantly greater than the entry risk.

The important components of the method are the following:

1. The market should show a clear level of support and resistance, defined by at least one visual anchor point on the chart

for both the support and resistance. Each anchor point should be a point that is visually separated from the trading days before and after it.

2. There should be a significant price difference between these support and resistance levels.

3. The market should return to test the support level. This can be either a breakout through the support on the downside or a test of the support that comes close to the support levels.

4. The market should demonstrate a clear bounce off the support levels.

5. The trade should be taken anticipating the cycle turning from a series of down days to a series of up days.

6. The trade should be taken respecting the overall market cycle.

Let's consider how this ideal model fits into the real world. Recall the Cisco (CSCO) chart we used to illustrate support and resistance in Chapter 4. In Figure 6.2, notice how a trader can use the support line to anticipate a move toward the upside after the rebound off the support level at $17.80.

Notice that, after leaving the price labeled Support, the stock price climbs to about $19.40, or more than half the distance from the support to the line labeled Resistance, at $20. This is not as high as I would prefer in the ideal case. Ideally, the price would rise again to near the resistance level, at $20. This trade is not a textbook example; few real-world examples are. Nevertheless, the rise to $19.40 is significant and sufficient for our case because it provides vertical and horizontal separation for the low labeled Support, which makes it a visual anchor point and one that is more likely to serve as a support level.

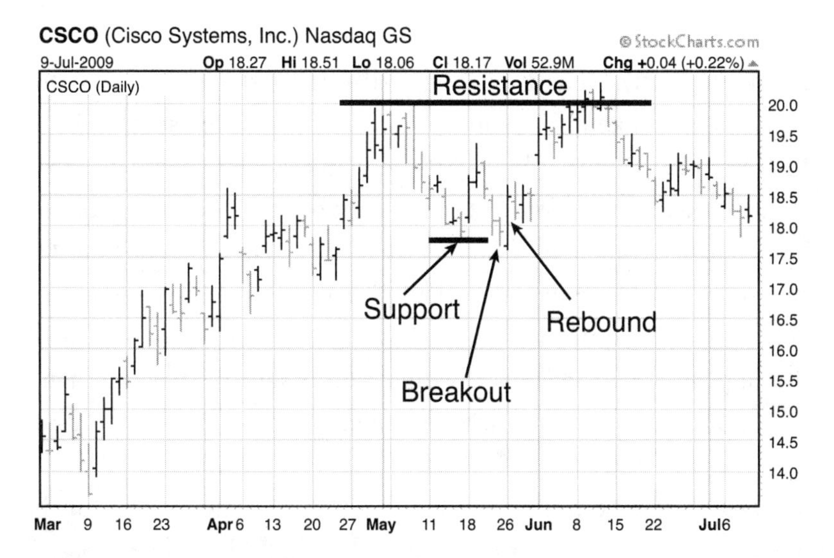

FIGURE 6.2 A swing rebound

This illustrates the requirement of a rally after the support point. *The support point needs to be something that other traders will see.* It must serve the psychological purpose of a price point that will bring buying pressure as the price approaches that price level again. A low followed by a significant rally when viewed visually on the chart will do that. Traders will expect a potential rally off of support if the price level that defines that support is visually significant on the daily chart. *The point must stand out visually.* This is the reason for a level of vertical (price) and horizontal (time) separation.

Therefore, the rally to $19.40 is the beginning of the setup for the rebound swing method because the bounce upward at $17.80 to about $19.30 creates a pivot point on the chart that will be support if the price drops again. The rally lasts a few days and is followed by a decline of two days.

The second time that the price drops back to the point labeled Breakout on the chart, we have the second condition of the rebound: a breakout or an approach very close to the support level. In this case, the price breaks through the support, so we have a breakout instead of just a test of the support. All else being equal, a breakout is better than a bounce that does not go lower than the support level: Any traders who had placed stops just below the support level are now out of the market because those stops were hit. A rise in price after the stops have been hit is slightly stronger than a rise in price without those stops having been hit.

Then at the point labeled Rebound, we have the trigger for the trade: a price that breaks the previous day's high. This price is significantly above the support level when measuring the distance between the support and resistance. When you have the breakout, you know the high price, so you can place an order to buy just above this high. If the order is filled, you know you will have a trade that meets the criteria of the rebound swing method.

In this particular case, I consider the break above the previous day's high to be a significant rise above the support level. One way to measure this quickly is to eyeball it. Those of you who prefer a more concrete guideline could pick a certain percentage to start. Over time, you, too, will be able to eyeball these price levels. For example, because the support was at $17.80 and the resistance was $20, the difference is $2.20. So a price above $17.80 plus 22¢, or $18.02, is 10% over the support. According to my eyeball of "significant price rebound," or the concrete definition of 10% higher, when the price on May 26 breaks the previous day's high, this triggers an entry for the rebound swing method trade.

Note how this trade also respects the cyclical nature of CSCO stock trading. The support level was originally set at the bottom of a down cycle. This was followed by a couple of up days that reached a high of about $19.30. Then the market cycle reversed and started trading down for three days in a row. The trade made on the 26th represents the first day of a potential up cycle. This increases the likelihood that the trade will be successful.

In Figure 6.3, I inset a portion of the chart for the S&P 500 stock market index below the prices for CSCO. You can see how the overall market cycles coincide very nicely with the CSCO market cycles. Most stocks are very highly correlated with the performance of the overall market. Therefore, you need to make sure that the overall market cycle is aligned with the cycle of the particular stock you want to trade before you enter a new position.

Note how a support level in the S&P prices gives the S&P a platform for a bounce, too. This means that this swing trade will be more likely to work, the overall market cycle has been going down and just turned up, the individual Cisco stock cycle has been going down for a few days and has just turned up, and the up cycle coincides with a bounce off of support for both the overall market and the individual stock. The confluence of these four events represents the perfect circumstances for a rebound swing method trade.

Although it's an excellent setup for the rebound swing method, this trade would not have been easy on the trader's psyche. After the entry at $18.15 or so on the 26th, the price went up substantially but then bounced around for the next three days between $18.10 and $18.70 before finally blasting up to $19.70 on June 1. The three days before it shot up would have been difficult for many traders; watching significant profits erode, then come back, and then erode again can be emotionally trying.

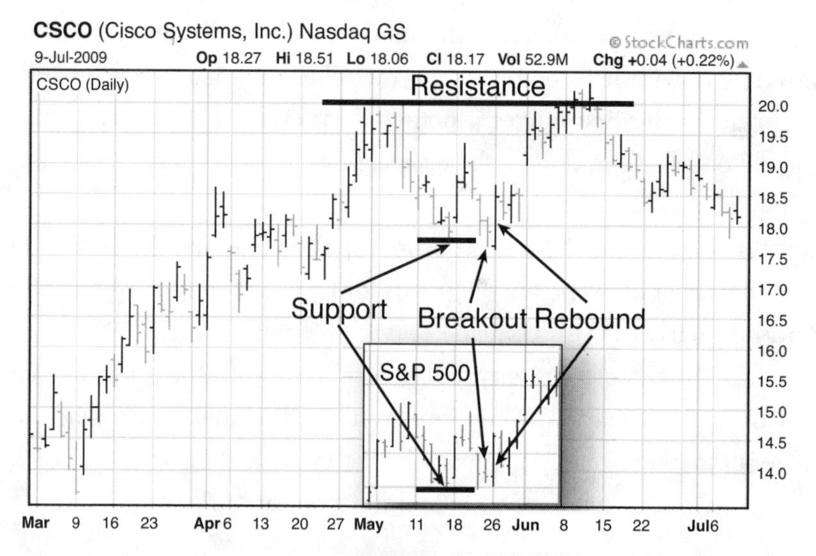

FIGURE 6.3 Overall market synchronization

As with many swing trades, the rebound swing method has a very short leash for the exit. You put on a stop just past the low of the current breakout. For this example, that would be a price below the low of $17.61 set on the 26th—approximately $17.50. This stop gets you out if the trade doesn't work out.

After the trade moves more than halfway to the resistance line, you should have a significant profit. If that happens, you should exit when the price breaks down a little bit. One easy method is to put a stop at the previous day's low so you will exit if the price drops below that price. This approach lets you continue to ride a long move if it continues in the same direction, but will get you out quickly in the event of a reversal. If you used this rule in the Cisco example, you would have exited on June 3 at a price just below $19.41. So you would have earned about $1.25 for a risk of about 55¢–60¢.

Now I break the method into its four components so that I can specifically address the role played by left-brain smarts and right-brain intuition in the trading of this method.

Market Environment

This method works well in many types of markets. However, you trade only long and short in a range-bound market. In a rising market, you trade only long trades. In a falling market, you trade only short trades.

The easiest way—and the most effective, from my experience—to determine the type of market is to open a daily chart that holds six months of prices. If the prices appear to be going down, then you are in a declining market. If they appear to be going up, then you are in a rising market. Suppress the left-brain need to have a very specific definition when making this judgment. Look at the chart and decide within a second or so: up, down, or sideways. If the answer is up, take only long trades; if the answer is down, take only short trades; and if the answer is sideways, you can take both kinds of trades.

This factor applies to both the market overall and individual stocks. If the overall market is down, don't trade buys off of support, no matter how an individual stock appears. These trades are more likely to fail if the market drags the individual stock down. If the overall market is up, don't short stocks off of resistance, for the same reason.

Setup

The setup for the trade is clearly established support and resistance that represents a significant price differential between these two levels. The easiest way to determine this is, again, with your eyeballs, using your right brain's pattern matching. Look at the chart and determine whether a particular stock has clear support and resistance. If it doesn't, move on to another stock. If it does, check the price differential between the support and the resistance. A stock needs room to run if it does bounce. This is a judgment call that you need to learn to make.

I like to see a potential profit of two to four times the entry risk. You should know the entry risk when you place the order because you will already know the price of entry and the lowest price of the breakout or test of the support. If the distance from the entry point to the resistance is not at least twice that amount, don't even place the order.

You will be able to train your right brain to quickly process the information required to analyze both these criteria for entry, enabling you to quickly determine whether a stock is getting ready for the rebound swing method. If you rely on your left brain for this task, you will need hours to prepare for trading each day. Your right brain is well suited for this task. Your left brain? Not so much.

Triggering Event

The trigger for the rebound swing method is a significant rebound or pullback inside the range between support and resistance. This is something that you can eyeball with practice. If it does not look significant on the chart, then it is not significant. Let your visual impression be your guide. Hold the chart at arm's length (or sit back in your chair as you look at your computer) and let your gut be your guide. Is your first impression that a price going above the previous day's high is significant? If not, what price would be significant according to your eyeball? That should be where you place a stop to enter the market.

Again, this is a right-brain judgment without a "correct" answer. You can train your right brain to recognize what is significant—which I address in the next chapter—but you can't easily describe it in rules that your left brain will understand.

Exit Event

The exit is easier. You are looking for one of two things: Either the trade works out and moves more than halfway toward the resistance, in which case you will exit when the momentum breaks down and the price drops below the previous day's low; or the trade won't work out and you will exit when the price drops to the stop price that was placed just below the support level.

Rebound Again

These patterns show up fairly regularly. After I wrote Chapter 4 with the original example of support and resistance, the market once again presented a rebound swing trade for CSCO. Figure 6.4 illustrates how this one turned out even better.

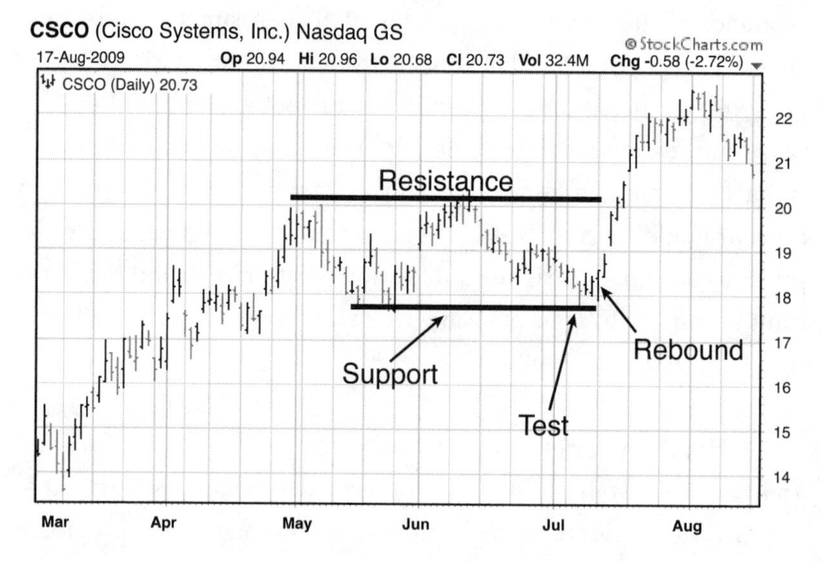

FIGURE 6.4 The second rebound swing trade for CSCO

The old adage "Cut your losses short and let your profits run" holds true even for shorter-term swing trading.

Although this is very simple and easy to understand, notice how the exit strategy of placing a stop just below the previous day's low after the price moved about halfway to the resistance would have kept you in the entire move from about $18.50 to $21.75, for a profit of about $3.25. Very simple swing-trading methods are similar to this. They generally won't turn out this well, but you will be able to ride a few big swings when the market moves your way while you are in the trade. The occasional large profit such as this one is not required for you to be successful in your trading, but it shows why the old adage "Cut your losses short and let your profits run" holds true even for shorter-term swing trading.

I have shown my personal rationale for one method and how you can use right-brain intuition in trading a specific method. In Chapter 7, "Simplicity and Speed: Training to Be a Master," I show how you can practice with intention to train your right brain to perform more effectively. In particular, I examine the "fuzzy" aspects of the rules for the rebound swing method and show how you can use your right brain to quickly analyze other "fuzzy" concepts. Your right brain was built for it.

CHAPTER 7

Simplicity and Speed: Training to Be a Master

"Excellence is an art won by training and habituation. We do not act rightly because we have virtue or excellence, but we rather have those because we have acted rightly. We are what we repeatedly do. Excellence, then, is not an act, but a habit."

—Aristotle

Richard Dennis—at the very height of his fame for having turned $10,000 into an estimated $200 million—gave 12 strangers only two weeks of training in his methods in year one of the Turtle experiment. Then after only 20 days of practice trading—for many of us, it was the only trading we had ever done—he gave us millions of dollars of his money to trade. The following year, he again trained some new traders, but he reduced the training to a single week. The amount of left-brain knowledge that one can impart in a single week is fairly limited. Dennis obviously did not believe that trading was complicated.

The lessons he taught us in the class can be boiled down to four simple rules:

1. **Trade with an edge**—Make sure that you have a trading strategy that will make money.
2. **Manage risk**—Don't trade with so much leverage that you risk losing everything.
3. **Be consistent**—Do this to reap the benefits of your trading strategy.
4. **Keep it simple**—Don't try to make trading more complicated than it actually is.

I described the specific strategy in less than 30 written pages in a bonus chapter of *Way of the Turtle.* Dennis and his trading partner, William Eckhardt, taught us this strategy in only a few days of the two-week training course.

As a Turtle, I simplified it even further.

For the first several months of the Turtle program—my first time doing actual trading of any sort—I studiously plotted the closing prices on the newspaper-sized "Commodity Perspective" paper charts we received each week. Then I realized that most of this was wasted work. What mattered was only whether the price made a new high or low, whether it broke out of the trading range. A price that didn't create a new high or low wasn't really relevant to our trading style. It was noise. So I stopped plotting noise. Simpler was better.

We were supposed to buy on breakouts of 10- to 12-week highs and sell short on breakouts of 10- to 12-week lows. After a while, I stopped counting the number of weeks because I found that I could eyeball the charts; my intuition told me that the most important factor was what the chart looked like, not whether it was a 9-week and 4-day breakout or a 10-week breakout. Again I simplified. Simpler was better.

It didn't take long before I spent almost no actual time deciding what to do. I looked at the price, looked at the chart, and knew immediately what to do. I didn't have to think. I had trained my right brain to do the thinking instantaneously.

If you had looked at what I was doing using left-brain analysis, you would have found out that I was, in fact, trading according to the rules we had been given, even though I was not using the left brain to make my trading decisions. I had trained my right brain to automate the left-brain tasks. This way was much quicker and just as accurate. I was able to do this because the actual left-brain knowledge required to trade our method—and most other methods that work in trading—is relatively small, deceptively small.

Unnecessary Complication

The great irony of trading is that it is difficult precisely because it is so very simple.

The great irony of trading is that it is difficult precisely because it is so very simple.

Our left brain often has a real problem with this concept. It doesn't make sense to the logical top-down left brain that it is simple to make money trading. Our logical mind imagines that if trading were simple, more traders would be successful; therefore, trading must be complicated. The left brain measures expertise in terms of only the type of knowledge that it values: categorizations, classifications, causal relationships, and temporal correlations—logical knowledge. The left brain assumes that trading requires a lot of its type of knowledge. It also assumes that a lot of analytical complication is required to trade well.

The great irony of trading is that it is difficult precisely because it is so very simple.

The left brain doesn't realize that the relative lack of attention to the right brain's importance in trading, not the lack of information, makes trading difficult for most people. The left brain doesn't put sufficient value on qualities that are the right brain's domain: big-picture perspective, bottom-up thinking, and pattern matching. These skills are required to become a master trader.

Most people are missing right-brain instinct and the confidence to trust that instinct. Hopefully earlier chapters offer a good framework for helping your left brain understand the importance of intuition and the right brain's bottom-up approach to thinking. Through proper training, you can build on this framework to help increase your left brain's trust in the right brain's capabilities. Through practice and habituation, you will soon learn to trust your gut as much as you trust your head and to trust your unconscious mind as much as you do your conscious, directed one.

The left brain's lack of appreciation for the right brain's big-picture expertise can be a source of major problems. The left brain feels a deep conflict when presented with the simple truths of trading success. It wants tricks and expertise that it can understand. It wants complication.

This is the reason so many traders seek gurus. Their logical brains don't believe that trading can be simple, so they try to seek out the hidden knowledge that must be missing from their trading. Lacking this secret information, traders often are hesitant and unconfident in their trading. The internal conflict between what their left brain tells them is required and the simple truth that trading is actually very simple undermines this confidence. So traders seek out others who can tell them what they think they must be missing. They believe that if they get the secret information, they will know enough to trade confidently.

Despite what some people might tell you, no secrets are involved. The art of the trade comes from simplicity, not complication, and from seeing the big picture.

Training the Right Brain

Master traders have learned to be comfortable with the simplicity of trading because they have trained their right brains to see the big picture—the forest as well as the trees. Master traders know that when they have prepared well, they can trust their decisions to their intuition and gut. They are comfortable letting their right brain dominate in certain types of decisions.

Master traders also know that many examples exist of simple phenomena that result in seemingly complex patterns. They are familiar with the way that markets display emergent behavior, and they have trained their right brains to recognize the signs of possible turns in market behavior at the earliest moment. They are able to respond to the market as it changes because they do not have their ego tied up in some rational prediction of what the market will do. They care only about what the market has done and what that means for their present course of action. The exact form the future will take is unknowable, and master traders are comfortable with that.

So how does a master trader train his right brain? In a word: practice.

As in artificial neural networks that need to be trained to pattern-match effectively, real neural networks in the right brain also need to be trained. This training should come in two different areas: pattern matching and environmental characterization. You need to train the right brain to recognize the patterns you seek to find for your trading, and you need to train the right brain so it can see the big-picture relationships among all the various market data.

The best practice for trading is trading itself. This is one of the reasons I recommend swing trading. You get a lot of opportunities to consider trades. Because you are concerned with market behavior during a much shorter period of time, you get more practice. Every time you make a decision to take a trade or pass, you are practicing. Even when the markets are slow, you can generally find opportunities to trade several times a month. This provides much more training than a longer-term trading style in which you might trade only a few times a year and good trades might last for months.

Fortunately, the typical process for trading is one that offers excellent practice for the right brain. Most of you already utilize a process such as the following one, which means you understand that how you approach each step is more important than the steps themselves. The essential steps for this common process are the following:

1. **Analyze the market state**—Determine whether it is a good time to consider purchases, short sales, or neither.
2. **Hunt for good stocks**—Find stocks that fit the strategy you are trading, and that reflect good potential buys or sells that harmonize with the overall market state.
3. **Determine the required trigger behavior**—Determine what each stock will have to do before you would buy or sell it; set appropriate market alerts so you will know if this behavior occurs.
4. **Prepare and execute orders**—Prepare the entry and exit criteria and quantity for any trades so that you are ready to place an order if an alert triggers. If an alert does trigger, check the overall market again and then place the order.

It might not be obvious at first glance, but when all four steps are done properly, the right brain has an opportunity to practice. This is true even of steps 3 and 4, which appear to be entirely left-brain activities.

In the next few sections, I break down the different steps, show the goal for each step, show how each step provides practice, and show a recommended approach for each step.

Analyze the Market State

The first step in the trading process each day is to consider the market state. With this step, you look to see if the market is good for initiating buys, initiating short sales, or neither. The key is that you are looking for times when it is good to be initiating a trade. You are not trying to figure out if the market is heading up or down. You are trying to read the market, not necessarily trying to predict it.

The best swing trades are initiated when the market exhibits all the following criteria:

- **Early in the market cycle**—The best condition for the market is when it is just starting to move in a particular direction after having moved some number of days in the opposite direction. You will be aligned to catch the next overall market cycle.
- **Technical alignment**—These are technical factors that increase the odds of a move in the desired direction. You must consider price-level support and resistance; potential support or resistance off other technical indicators that other

market participants follow, such as trend lines or moving averages; and support and resistance near round-number price levels.

- **Running room**—These are technical factors that increase the odds that the market will move a significant amount if it does move in the desired direction. For a buy, you are looking for a lack of resistance near the purchase-price level. For a sell, you are looking for a lack of support near the purchase level.

Doing this well requires using the right brain, especially the spatial relationship manipulation and imagination that the right brain excels at. You need to be able to perform what-if analysis in your head. You are not concerned with what the market tells you right now. Instead, you are concerned with what the market will be telling you if some significant change takes place. For example, what would it mean if the S&P rises 15 points today? Is the market starting a new up cycle? Is it bouncing off support? Is it bouncing off a trend line? Is it likely to run into resistance?

Figure 7.1 illustrates some analysis points. Remember to consider the points as if the trading days that followed were not yet there.

- **Potential buy A**—This scenario is a day following a significant down move that was a few days down, a few days up, and then one day down a lot and one day that appeared to stabilize on the support around the 900 price level. At this point, a day that broke the previous day's high would represent a potential start of an up cycle and the potential start of a rebound off the support, at 900. Reasonable running room would also be available because the price could go to at least 925 before hitting resistance, and perhaps as high as 950. So the opportunity for a 3%–6% swing in the market is relatively high.

FIGURE 7.1 Market state analysis

- **Potential buy B**—This scenario is a day following a significant drop in which three of the last four days were down days and the price appeared to find some support at the 875–880 level. A move above the high of the day that made the low would represent a potential cycle reversal and rebound off the support, at 875. A lot of running room would also be available at this price because potential resistance at 925 is about 5% away and potential resistance at 950 is about 8% away.

- **Potential sell A**—In this scenario, the price has reached the resistance level at 950 after several very significant up days. A drop below the low of the previous day's low would represent a potential rebound off the 950 resistance and the potential beginning of a new down cycle.

It is important to note that the potential sell would have remained valid for each of the successive days if the market had dropped lower. However, this did not happen. This illustrates an important aspect of the what-if analysis of swing trading. Four days would have represented good days for a sell if the market had done something. However, it did not trigger the action that would have made a good sale, so you would not have actually made any short-swing sales during this time because the market triggers were not met. The market conditions were ready, but the market did not indicate the beginning of a down cycle.

So in this particular what-if scenario, the "if" condition did not occur, which is why this is considered a potential sell point. It had the potential to indicate a market sell condition if certain things had occurred, primarily if the price of the S&P 500 Index had dropped below the previous day's low.

- **Potential buy C**—In the case of the "Potential Buy C" point, significant downward retracement off the highs at approximately 1,020 has occurred, and there is running room of about 3% from the previous day's high, at approximately 990. So a market move above this 990 high represents a potential start of an up cycle that could run to approximately 1,020.
- **No buy point**—This point corresponds with the point labeled "NO Buy" on the chart. In contrast with "Potential Buy C," this point does not follow a significant retracement. It also shows only about 1% running room, so the market could easily run into resistance very quickly. Therefore, a significant up move in the market is less likely.

Remember that the goal when analyzing the market state is to be able to answer these two questions: What, if anything, would the market have to do for it to be a good time to initiate a buy? And what, if anything, would the market have to do for it to be a good time to initiate a sell? If the market can't do anything on a given day to indicate that it is a good time to buy or sell, you should just wait for another day to do your trading. Most of the time, I find this to be the case. Most days are not good days to initiate a swing buy or sell.

Most days are not good days to initiate a swing buy or sell.

To train your right brain properly, you need to make this analysis very quickly. Don't allow time for your left brain to take over. At first, give yourself less than 15 seconds to answer with one of these: "Buy if it exceeds yesterday's high," "Sell if it drops below yesterday's low," or "Neither." As you gain practice, reduce the time you have to make this decision.

Keep your analysis visual instead of numerical. Doing this quickly and visually forces you to use your gut intuition instead of your intellect. Use a stopwatch if you find yourself unable to make a decision quickly. If you reach the time limit without making a decision, the answer is "neither" by default.

Over time, you should be able to glance at a chart of the major indices and decide in less than one second if the criteria for a buy or sell have been met. You will need to do this as a last-minute check just before placing your orders to buy or sell the stock. If you can make this decision quickly, you are using your gut.

Remember Juan Fangio. If you don't have time to think, your intuition will take over. So don't give yourself time to think while you are practicing. Force your intuition to take over.

Hunt for Good Stocks

The search for good stocks depends on the particular method you are using. Many different swing-trading methods work. In the hunt for a stock that meets the criteria of the system, your right brain will help immensely. Most traders use a combination of computer automation and right-brain pattern matching to narrow the choice of stocks on which to focus for their methods. This is the most efficient way for most methods. Use the computer to help you quickly cycle through a set of charts.

You will monitor three classes of stocks:

1. **Tradable stocks**—Stocks that are liquid and priced at a level that is appropriate for your account balance
2. **Stocks to watch**—Stocks that are tradable and that represent potential trades if they move in the right direction
3. **Potential trades**—Stocks that are close enough that you will place orders if the overall market conditions match

In the previous chapter, I used the rebound swing method as one example of a swing-trading method. I use that same example here to illustrate how you would use your right brain to determine the list of stocks to watch.

With the rebound swing method, you are looking for stocks with well-defined support and resistance levels. This is a fuzzy, subjective concept—exactly the kind of concept the right brain was built for.

As I look for stocks that would make good rebound swing trades, I use my eyes and my right brain to make the subjective analysis very quickly: Does a well-defined band of support and resistance exist? This is a simple question with a yes or no answer. If the answer is yes, that stock goes on the watch list. If the answer is no, the stock stays off the list, and I make a note to reexamine that stock in a week or so to see if it will then meet the criteria.

If it takes you time to answer, you are not using your intuition; you are using your intellect.

The answer to the important question of whether to put the stock on the list should arrive immediately. As with judging the market condition, if it takes you time to answer, you are not using your intuition; you are using your intellect. You can't train your gut if you are using your smarts instead. So you need to force yourself to answer the question quickly. Don't worry about being wrong. Just answer the question in less than a second. Does well-defined support and resistance exist? If you can't tell, it means no; either it isn't there or it is not well defined. If you don't get an immediate yes, it means no. Go on to the next stock.

Determine the Required Trigger Behavior

After you have selected your stocks to watch, the next step is to determine what it would take for you to actually buy or sell each stock—to "trigger" a buy or sale.

With this step, you are looking to narrow the stocks to watch to an even smaller set, those that are close enough to being a buy or sell that you should set a market alert to tell you when the price exceeds or drops below a certain level. You are trying to decide whether you should buy, sell, or neither. Again, this step is ideally suited to gut intuition because it is based on subjective soft criteria. So to train the gut, focus on arriving at the answer as quickly as possible.

Figure 7.2 illustrates a graph using the criteria for the rebound swing method.

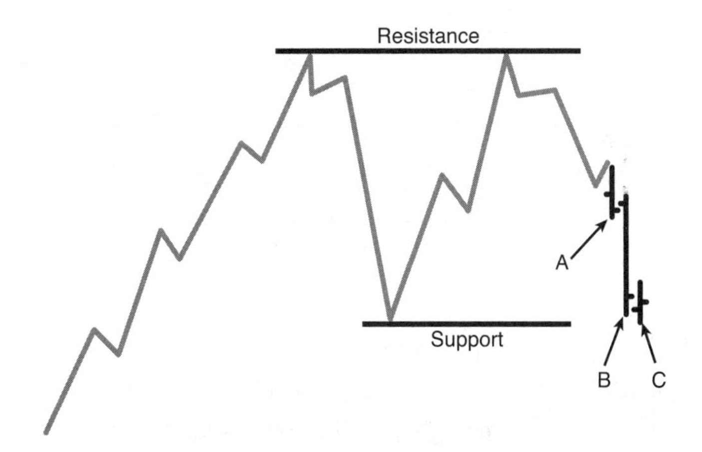

FIGURE 7.2 Determining trigger criteria

To meet the trigger criteria for the rebound swing method, the stock needs to represent a significant rebound off the support level and also have a profit potential that is two to four times the entry risk. Applying these criteria to the points on Figure 7.2, we see that breaking the high for bar A does not meet either of the criteria. No rebound occurs off the support, and the profit potential is about equal to the amount risked if you place your exit stop below the support.

A price that exceeds the high for bar B does represent a significant rebound off the support—too significant, it seems. By the time the price gets that high, it is very far away from the support level, which means the risk for the trade is too high. For this reason, bar B fails to meet the second criterion. The potential profit is not large enough compared to the risk; it shows only about a 1:1 ratio, whereas we are looking for between 2:1 and 4:1.

Notice how bar C meets both criteria. A price that exceeds the high of bar C is a significant rebound, and the potential profit is about five or six times the risk if the price rises all the way to the resistance level.

Your right brain doesn't care about numbers; it cares about the relationships between the bars, which can be represented without any numbers.

I didn't place any prices on this chart for a reason. They are not necessary, and they will mess up the training for your gut intuition. Your right brain doesn't care about numbers; it cares about the relationships between the bars, which can be represented without any numbers. You should have already decided that the distance between the support and resistance is large enough during the previous step while hunting for good stocks, so you don't need the numbers anymore.

With a bit of practice, you can quickly determine whether you should set a price alert for a stock. It shouldn't take more than a second or two. If you can't say yes in a few seconds, don't set the alert. It's as simple as that.

Prepare and Execute Orders

After you have set your alerts, you have a little time to relax. You can then go through the charts to determine the exact exit stop prices you want to use if any particular alert goes off. This determines your exact risk level, which you can use to determine your quantity. Use whatever position-sizing methods you are comfortable with (see the "Bibliography" if you need help determining the best position-sizing algorithm).

Choosing the stop price is another subjective task when using the rebound swing system. You want to set it just below the support level. This might be a somewhat fuzzy line as prices dip through and around previous support. Pick a line visually that you think represents the support, and then pick a price point below it. Again, do this visually, forcing yourself to use your right brain for this task. Then find the actual price on the side of the chart. Alternately, you can use the highs and lows for particular days to help you determine the exact price. Just remember that you want to pick the price level quickly and visually first with your gut intuition, and then determine the exact price using your analytical left brain.

If you have prepared properly, you should have all the information at hand to enter an order with your broker when an alert goes off. Before you enter an order, you should run one last check. Make sure that the overall market has met your criteria for entry. Checking the overall market should take less than a few seconds if you have a 5-minute, 15-minute, or hourly chart handy.

With the swing rebound method, you don't want to have an order execute if the market has not yet indicated that it is a good time to buy or sell. If the market is close to reaching its price criterion but has not yet met it, you can set an alert and wait until the alert for the index triggers before you place your orders.

Keep It Simple and Quick

The key to engaging your gut intuition during your practice is to force yourself to keep it simple and quick. This might appear to be an oversimplification, but I have found that most traders overcomplicate things, letting their left brains dominate where their gut intuition would serve them far better.

If you have to make decisions quickly, you won't have time to overcomplicate the picture with unnecessary analysis. If you don't have to do complicated analysis, it's easier to be quick. Simplicity enables speed, and speed forces simplicity.

Confine yourself to very specific goals when practicing. Recall how each of the four steps had a very specific question or two that you are trying to answer: Is the market ready for initiating a buy? Does a stock have well-defined support and resistance levels? Would a stock have significantly rebounded off the support if it exceeds yesterday's high? Is that high low enough that room still exists to make a profit before the price reaches the resistance level?

You can quickly answer each of these questions with a glance at the chart when you have practiced using your intuition to make these decisions. You practice by limiting the amount of time you allow yourself for analysis, which keeps you from overcomplicating the decision process.

You become a master trader by practicing as if you already are a master trader. Master traders make decisions quickly, so you need to make the decisions quickly during your practice. Just remember that if you are in doubt, the answer is no. You can always answer no quickly.

Simplicity and speed are signs of the master trader.

CHAPTER 8

Techno Traders

"One machine can do the work of 50 ordinary men.
No machine can do the work
of one extraordinary man."

—Elbert Hubbard

A few years ago, my friend Astrid sent me an e-mail asking if I wanted to join her skydiving team for some practice sessions in the SkyVenture vertical wind tunnel in Orlando, Florida.

A vertical wind tunnel is a round chamber 12 feet in diameter with a coarse screen mesh at the floor to let wind through, and again at the top, about 20 feet off the ground. Several enormous electric fans at the top of the tunnel suck wind through the chamber at speeds of more than 120 miles per hour (or a bit less than 200 kilometers per hour).

This speed is known as **terminal velocity**, the speed at which the drag from the wind against your body equals the force of gravity so you stop accelerating. If you jump off a stationary object, such as a helicopter or an air balloon, you will reach terminal velocity in only a few seconds, and then the rest of your freefall will be at this same speed. In a wind tunnel operating at terminal velocity, you can float in the air and appear motionless to someone looking in from the windows on the side.

Skydiving teams often practice using a wind tunnel because it is cheaper than jumping from planes for each minute of flying time, and it is possible to get many minutes flying in rapid succession. When you are jumping out of actual airplanes, it takes considerable time for the plane to climb to altitude, for it to glide down to a landing after you pull your chute, and for you to pack your chute after you land. If you are really fast and have two chutes, you might be able to get 7–10 jumps in a day. With the wind tunnel, you just jump into the wind stream and you are flying. It takes only a few seconds.

Astrid's team booked the wind tunnel in several hour segments during the course of a few days and needed some friends to fill the time between their practice sessions. They would get too tired if they practiced nonstop with no rests between sessions, so she wanted to know if I'd be willing to share the time with them. She also offered to give me free coaching. Astrid is a world-class formation flyer, so this was an offer I couldn't refuse.

Before I joined them at the wind tunnel, I had been skydiving for about a year and a half. I had about 165 jumps out of airplanes, but I had been practicing skydiving for less than three total hours. Because each jump generally lasts a minute or less, depending on the type of jump, I had less than 165 minutes of total freefall time.

Before I actually experienced freefall myself, it appeared that flying around in the air would be pretty easy. After I jumped, I found out that it is much more difficult than it looks. At 120 miles per hour, the wind has a lot of power. If you stick out one leg slightly more than the other, you will flip over or spin very rapidly. You can easily lose consciousness if you spin too fast because the blood will flow out to your hands and feet, leaving your brain without enough oxygen. Skydiving can be dangerous.

At the point I joined Astrid's team at the wind tunnel, I could pretty easily maintain control, but I was still flying using my conscious intellect. I had to deliberately control parts of my body to move around in the air. If I wanted to move up, I knew to spread out my body so that I presented more surface area to the wind. If I wanted to move down, I knew to bring my legs and arms closer to my body to reduce the drag. If I wanted to turn, I knew I could tilt my hands to the left or the right to create a turning force. I was competent, but slow and deliberate. I was not an intuitive flyer.

After spending the first day in the wind tunnel, I got comfortable with the particulars of the tunnel. It was harder to fly in the tunnel than in the smoother air outside a plane. You had to be more precise. Astrid and her team members taught me a few tricks. I learned how to use my legs to turn more rapidly. I learned to stay away from the edges of the tunnel where the eddies in the wind current were located.

But then Astrid suggested that we play a game. Instead of worrying about what to do, I only had to follow her around as she would tag some point on the side of the tunnel wall. First, she might tag a low spot near the cable-mesh floor. Then she'd tag another spot on the other side of the tunnel a bit higher. Then she might tag a spot much higher up. Following her required that I use everything I had learned to turn and go up and down as rapidly as possible.

Sometimes I had to turn halfway around and drop. Sometimes I had to turn one-quarter and back up. I had to keep Astrid in view as I went so that I could quickly move to the next spot. Besides being great training, it was a lot of fun. As fast as I could go, Astrid was always just a little bit faster, leading me and urging me to go just a little faster.

After a few more hours during which I played this game for perhaps 15–20 minutes total, something surprising happened. I stopped having to think about what to do. My actions became unconscious, intuitive. I was no longer flying with my left brain—I was using my whole mind. After I made this transition, I flew around the chamber at three or four times the speed that I could muster when I was using only my left brain. I had become an intuitive flyer.

Using some very expensive technology, I was able to speed up my learning to become an advanced skydiver in much less time that it would have taken under normal circumstances. The technology of the wind tunnel provided more practice and a more precise environment in which to learn flying skills. It enabled me to distill years of flying know-how and sensation into a few short days of experience.

Master traders use technology to keep their skills sharp and their intuition honed to a fine edge.

Master traders use technology for analogous reasons. They use it to keep their skills sharp and their intuition honed to a fine edge. They use it so that they can sift through hundreds or thousands of trading opportunities during a time period when they might previously have been able to sort through only tens. They use it to speed up their learning. They are ready to act on any opportunities the market brings.

Techno Trading

I started programming trading systems using an Apple II when I was still in high school. At the time, this was a cutting-edge use of technology. When I traded as a Turtle, our quote terminals contained only prices. They showed the high, low, last price, net change, and volume for each contract. That's it.

We had to draw our own graphs on paper. We didn't have intraday charts. We had to look at the prices and determine whether the price was significant using only memory and paper charts. Using a very simple trading method reduced the amount of information I needed to keep in my head.

Fortunately, the technology available to traders has tremendously advanced during the last 25 years. The modern master trader's tools are a fast computer, a fast and reliable Internet connection, a few large-screen monitors, and advanced trading software. Most traders have two or three computers: One they use only for trading, another they use for trading research, and sometimes another they use for e-mail and general Internet use.

Traders can use this technology to promote and sustain a healthy interplay between the left and right hemispheres. For example, when your intuition comes up with an idea, it's easy to test different aspects of trading ideas using computer software programs. For long-term trading, it is even possible to create completely automated trading systems that make money. For medium-term trading, it is a bit more difficult but still generally possible.

However, even with today's advanced technology, total automation is often impractical for short-term trading such as swing trading. The biggest reason is that a completely automated swing-trading strategy is beyond the programming capabilities of the vast majority of traders using the tools that are available to the retail trader. So you need to use a balance of your whole mind to properly test a potential short-term trading idea.

Consider the rebound swing method. Although it is easy to train your right brain to recognize whether a particular stock has clear support and resistance, this is a difficult concept to program into a computer. Support and resistance are concepts that are primarily based on visual perception. Does the support hold up if the price goes 25¢ below the previous low? How about 45¢? Does it make any difference if the previous support was only five days earlier? How about three days? How much price differential between the support and resistance is significant? These are all fuzzy concepts with fuzzy answers.

Computer programs want hard answers to specific questions. They don't like fuzzy concepts or fuzzy answers. Algorithmic computer programs are entirely left brain. They are annoyingly logical. They want to be told exactly what to do. They can't see the big picture. They can see the trees, but they don't know that a forest exists.

The important factor for the specific concepts of support and resistance is what other traders will perceive using their eyes.

The important factor for the specific concepts of support and resistance is what other traders will perceive using their eyes. Other traders' perceptions of support and resistance create the tendency for the price to rebound off support and resistance. If you can't accurately program a concept that duplicates other traders' perceptions, you won't be able to accurately test the method. The best retail trading computers and software programs cannot currently perform this task.

This is good because it means that traders who use a proper balance of intuition and intellect will be able to test and implement ideas that are profitable but that are not likely to be automated. The trading that exists just beyond the reach of technology offers better opportunity for those who have properly trained their gut intuition to excel. If it were easy to create a computer program that could duplicate your intuition, more computers would be trading and less opportunities would be available for the individual trader without the banks of hyperfast computers that Goldman Sachs might have available.

This is also one of the reasons swing trading offers good potential for intuitive traders. It is beyond the reach of our current left brain-oriented computer technology.

Augmenting Intellect and Analysis

Nevertheless, even for intuitive whole-mind traders, software can be a useful tool. It can help the intellect validate components of the intuition's trading ideas. Most real-time charting software can also alert you to potential trades. It can help you filter the enormous amounts of information contained in historical market price data. Sophisticated backtesting software can test some less complex methods, and it can test pieces of intuitive trading concepts.

For example, you might not be able to program backtesting software to exactly recognize support and resistance, but you could test an approximation of parts of this idea to explore the profitability of the rebound swing method. Because testing software can't exactly capture the concept of support and resistance, the results from historical testing won't match what you might have achieved using your intuition. Nevertheless, these sorts of tests are useful because they often help you find weaknesses in a particular method that might not have been obvious from looking only at the charts.

For fuzzy concepts that are hard to capture exactly, I use historical testing tools to test ideas that are approximations of the fuzzy concept. I try as many approximate rule sets as I can come up with. If they all test well and in similar ways, this is a good sign that the fuzzy intuitive concept itself is valid. If you try several different rule-based approximations for particular intuitive-entry concepts, and each of these approximations appears to demonstrate a significant trading edge, then you can have a lot more intellectual faith in your approach. So even though the concepts might be fuzzy and based on right-brain visual perception, you can use technology to explore the profitability of the ideas.

One of the best ways to do this test of parts is to separate the entry criteria from the rest of the method steps. I like to run tests that examine the amount the price moves in the trade's favor, as compared with how much it moves against the trade within a certain number of days after entry. In technical terms, I look for the maximum favorable excursion (MFE) adjusted for volatility, divided by the maximum adverse excursion (MAE) adjusted for volatility. I call this measure the **edge ratio**. After a test, this measure might indicate that within five days of the entry, a stock moves an average of two times as far in the desirable direction as it does in the undesirable direction. This measure gives you a pretty good feel for the opportunity for significant profit potential. If a stock moves significantly more in the desired direction after you enter than it does in the opposite direction for the first several days, this is a positive sign for a swing-trading system.

Another approach that works is to test entry ideas using a very simple exit strategy such as the one I suggested for the rebound swing method. Then you can examine the profitability of the trades using the approximate entry criteria. If these trades are profitable, this should give you greater intellectual confidence in the fuzzy method that the entry rules attempt to approximate.

An additional valuable technique is to visually examine all the trades that meet the approximate conditions. This enables you to see how well your approximate rules match the fuzzy idea you are trying to model. When you can see the trades themselves, you can get a more intuitive feel for how the concept you are analyzing works. This procedure might also give you ideas for how you can improve the approximation. Sometimes it also suggests ways to improve the overall method.

This is one of the ways intellect and analysis can validate intuition. If you can use software tools to help your analysis, that's even better. Just remember, if it is too easy a concept to program into the computer, other people likely will have found the idea, making it potentially less profitable.

Augmented Intuition Training

Computer technology is not just for the left brain. It is also valuable in training intuition. Similar to how the wind tunnel helped me cram years of skydiving into a few days of intense practice, a computer program can help you train your intuition by speeding up the learning process.

Trading software can help automate the process of training the right brain by quickly presenting you with visual stock and market charts. Modern charting software lets you easily set up specific filter screens of charts that meet specific criteria. For example, you could find all stocks that are below their 40-day high and above their 40-day low, all stocks that have made all-time highs, all stocks trading between $5 and $20, or any number of other criteria. Many of the more popular retail brokerage firms offer their customers free software that has these features. These tools are common and powerful.

Utilizing charting and screening software, you can quickly sort through hundreds of charts, using your right brain's visual perception system to quickly determine whether a particular stock meets your selection criteria. You can then add stocks that you want to keep closer track of to an electronic watch list. These lists let you periodically filter the stocks to find those that are close to meeting your trading criteria. This will save you time and enable you to effectively scan a much larger set of stocks to trade.

This is one area where getting the right software can pay large dividends. Mediocre software lets you watch a small list of stocks because it takes more time to find and analyze potential stocks. Good software lets you watch a much larger list of stocks for the same effort. This capability translates directly into more quality trading opportunities. Don't skimp on your trading software. Software that makes you more productive will make you more profitable.

The professional tools are sometimes better. And better can make a difference. If you want to be a professional, invest in professional tools where it matters. If it means moving to a different brokerage firm and paying a slightly higher price for your commissions or paying a monthly fee, the costs can be worth it for the right features.

Keeping Up

New trading technology comes out all the time, so master traders are constantly evaluating the latest tools. They are aware of the best tools, and they try out new technologies as they become available because they know that the right tools will help them use their intuition more effectively and with greater precision.

When used properly, technology becomes an extension and assistant to both the right and left hemispheres. It amplifies not only the capabilities of the intellect, but also those of the intuition.

When used properly, technology becomes an extension and assistant to both the right and left hemispheres. It amplifies not only the capabilities of the intellect, but also those of the intuition. It can also help you maintain the balance between your two minds because it can help you develop a trading process that uses each part of your brain most effectively.

Your left brain knows that the right brain is better at finding patterns, reading complex pictures, and seeing the forest for the trees. When you use technology to amplify the best skills of each part of your mind, you build trust between the hemispheres. Your gut can find patterns more effectively if it knows that the intellect will be there to serve as a backstop. You can be more confident in your trading when you have used technology to sort through years of data to hone your intuition.

Technology is just a tool, but it can be a powerful aid if you use it to develop balance as a trader.

CHAPTER 9

A Careful Balancing Act

"Well-bred instinct meets reason halfway."

—George Santayana

When I was young, I believed that my most important focus was controlling my emotions and living a life based on logical, reasoned principles. I attributed my early success in life to my intellect, my brains, and quite a bit of luck. I underestimated the value of my intuition.

When Stanley Angrist interviewed me about 20 years ago for *The Wall Street Journal* article he was writing about the Turtles, he asked me why I thought I had been so successful compared with many of the other Turtles. I answered that I thought it was because I had less fear, probably because of my younger age. I felt that some of the other Turtles had let their fear cause them to hesitate in their trading, especially in the beginning.

Over the years, I have changed my opinion of what accounted for my success as a Turtle. In my book, *Way of the Turtle,* I said that emotional and psychological strength were the most important ingredients in trading. I now believe that although this statement is true, it is incomplete and can even be misleading. I underestimated the value of my intuition.

It is not sufficient to be strong and tough, to have an intellectual sort of machismo. Trading is not a battle among the world's strongest traders. The source of the psychological confidence and strength matters. Traders who combine intellect and instinct—smarts and intuition—will have a much easier emotional ride. Traders who fight their gut instincts and let their left brains dominate when their right brains are screaming "No" will find it much harder to keep trading in the face of adversity.

I found it easy to trade as a Turtle because I followed my gut instinct. I was trading intuitively, so it wasn't difficult for me. Others who did not trust their instincts—who were looking for left-brain explanations for every possible action—had a much harder time.

It comes down to a level of trust. No matter how you prepare, if you don't trust your trading strategy, you won't be able to confidently execute your plan. You won't be able to display the "emotional and psychological strength" required to be a successful trader.

If I seemed to overemphasize intuition's role in trading in this book, it's because I believe that most traders underutilize their intuition and instincts, not because I believe that intuition alone can work, or even that intuition is superior to intellect.

Your reason and instinct must meet in the middle
and agree to complement each other
if you are to perform at your best.

Success requires a balance between your smarts and your intuition. It requires that you permit each part of your mind to do the job that it can best perform. Your reason and instinct must meet in the middle and agree to complement each other if you are to perform at your best. This is the middle way of trading.

Balancing Intuition

Your intuition is not infallible. It will make mistakes. It will send you on wild goose chases. It will find some patterns that appear to be very promising but that, on further investigation, don't turn out to be the gold mines they first seemed. You need your left brain's analytical nature to help direct your intuition in these cases, to correct it and steer it away from rocky shores. Analysis and intuition should work hand in hand, in balance.

The question remains, how should you create and maintain this balance? You can talk about balance, but you need to be able to put this concept into actual practice for it to do any good. An example from other fields might help illustrate the process.

Starting about 1985, research psychologist Gary Klein and a few colleagues were studying the way people such as firefighters, nurses, and military personnel actually made decisions. Their results were surprising. Before their research, Klein and his colleagues believed that the best way to make decisions involved a rational analysis in which the decision maker carefully weighed alternatives. Surprisingly, Klein and his fellow researchers found that expert firefighters, nurses, and military leaders did not make decisions by logically weighing alternatives. Instead, the vast majority *used their intuition.* Instead of comparing among alternatives, they acted intuitively and pattern-matched. Most of them said that they *didn't even have to think* about the right answers; they *just knew what to do.* They drew upon their experience with similar circumstances in the past and developed a primary plan of action almost immediately.

One aspect of his research particularly surprised Klein. He originally had thought that *novices* would impulsively choose the first plausible plan and that they would be less likely to evaluate among alternatives. He had expected that *experts* would evaluate several scenarios and base their decisions on an evaluation among these choices. He believed that because experts had more experience, they would be able to evaluate a greater array of potential scenarios.

Instead, he found the opposite. Experts almost immediately were primed toward *one particular course of action.* They then checked this course for viability, and if they found it viable, they acted on it. The experts intuited the right answer without having to think about it. Their right brain quickly built the answer in a bottom-up manner to arrive at a viable solution to the problem.

In contrast, the novices spent much more time in the decision-making process because they were carefully evaluating among competing alternatives. They did not have enough examples of similar prior events in their experience to enable them to quickly determine which alternative was clearly superior. The novices spent all their time using their intellect.

Experts used their intuition to arrive at an initial plan, and then they evaluated that plan for viability using their left brain's analysis.

It's important to notice that the experts used their *intuition to arrive at an initial plan,* and then they *evaluated that plan for viability using their left brain's analysis,* asking questions such as, Am I missing something? Do I have time for this approach? Is a safer alternative available? Will this approach work?

Intellect and intuition working hand in hand, each working at what it does best: This is the middle way of trading.

Klein's experts used their intuition to guide the direction of their intellect so that they did not waste time thinking about alternatives that were clearly inferior. In trading, intuition can also guide the process of strategy development. Then intellect can make sure that the strategies will work. And when you start trading, your intuition can take over again to recognize the patterns that make up the components of the trading strategy.

The proper interplay between intuition and intellect is the sign of a master trader.

Balance in Trading

An example of a healthy partnership between intellect and intuition in strategy development illustrates one way in which you can achieve this balance. Suppose that your right brain notices that a certain price pattern often precedes large up moves in many of the stocks you have been following. For the purposes of this example, suppose you noticed that an inside day followed by an outside day tends to precede a large move in the direction of the close of the outside day. Your intuition tells you to investigate a strategy in which you would buy if you had an inside day followed by an outside day that closed higher, and you would sell if you had an inside day followed by an outside day that closed lower.

Your intuition has *flagged an idea* as a potential trading strategy. Your left brain, being the natural skeptic, runs through its list of potential problems:

- **Visual perception bias**—Your intellect is aware of the visual perception's tendency to notice significant points on the chart and ignore points that are less visually significant. For traders, this often means that your eye is drawn to the prices that surround big moves and the patterns that precede them, but you might not even notice when the same pattern shows up inside a price consolidation. This will sometimes cause you to believe that the pattern is more significant than it really is.

To determine whether the pattern really represents a trading opportunity, your intellect knows that you must take a methodical approach to investigate that pattern. This might initially involve carefully analyzing some charts in which you use your left brain's attention to *carefully search* for the pattern in all the data. Then if the pattern still appears promising, you might use a backtesting application to run a historical analysis of the pattern. A properly programmed computer will *not* be susceptible to the same visual perception bias to which your right brain is vulnerable.

- **Not enough data**—Your intellect is aware that although your intuition might have found a pattern, the pattern might appear only in the relatively limited amount of data represented by the charts you have been looking at. Your left brain is aware of the need for a statistically significant sample size and of the way in which our intuition can be fooled because a pattern emerges a few times in a relatively short period of time.

  To validate the idea over more data, your intellect will move you to analyze more charts. You might try looking backward several more years to see if this pattern holds up. If the pattern still seems promising, you will likely want to run computer backtesting to analyze the pattern over a lot more data.

In this example, notice how the ideas that your intuition noted were used as the basis for more rigorous testing. This is as it should be. If you can satisfy your intellect that a strategy you have developed using your intuition is, in fact, valid and profitable, you will be able to trade it with full confidence. *Your whole mind* will be able to get behind the strategy, so your confidence trading it will be higher. This makes it much easier to display the emotional and psychological strength that distinguishes a master trader from the pack.

Living Mastery

When you are able to trade beyond your intellect and from your gut, you will find that trading requires less effort. You won't agonize over decisions. You won't spend as much time sorting through the same information. You will have more time and energy to devote to other tasks.

Mastery is a continuous process, a path instead of a destination.

Mastery is a continuous process, a path instead of a destination. The markets will change. Technology will change. Some things will become harder. Some things will become easier. The middle way will help you adapt to new environments, crises, and opportunities. You will more easily find opportunities and the means to exploit them.

When you find the middle way of the master trader, I suspect that you won't be satisfied with a purely rational approach to trading. You will prefer the speed and simplicity of the middle way.

Trading with your whole mind is simpler, faster, better, and more profitable.

CONCLUSION

The Art of the Trade

"The game taught me the game. And it didn't spare me the rod while teaching."

—Jesse Livermore

Trading…there is no substitute.

Practice helps. Computer research helps. Reading helps. Studying individual charts helps. But at the end of the day, there's no substitute for putting your money on the line and making actual trades.

The best way to begin the process is to open a trading account and put some real money at risk.

So whether you are an experienced trader with your own proven techniques who wants to learn to use your whole mind more effectively in your trading or a new trader who is just starting the learning process, the best way to begin the process is to open a trading account and put some real money at risk. This is the only way that you will be able to develop and condition your whole mind for the rigors of trading.

Unfortunately, learning is a process that inevitably involves a lot of failure. You won't learn if you don't risk enough to potentially fail. So you must take the plunge and be prepared to lose some money along the way.

Sometimes the big losses are the ones that teach you the most. I remember one trade in particular. It was 1987, the last full year of the Turtle program. Silver ran up from $11 to over $15 in about a month. Because we were breakout trend followers, we bought just as the price made new highs slightly above $11. In Figure C.1, you can see where we entered the trade and the subsequent price movement up until my exit point.

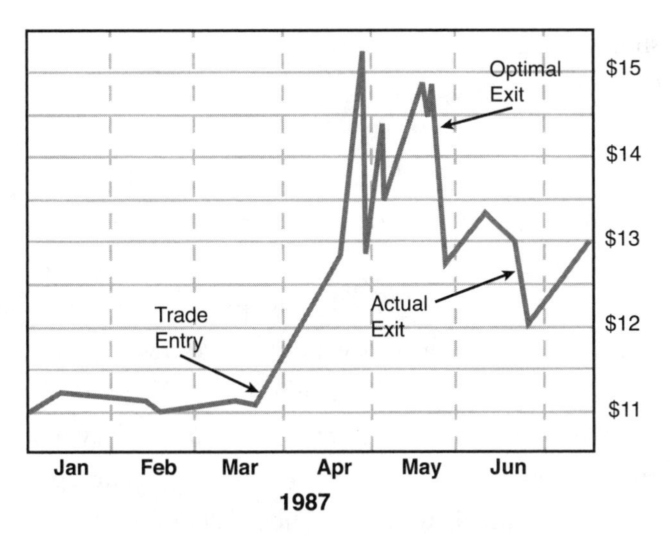

FIGURE C.1 The 1987 silver trade

Because I bought very low and exited the trade just above $12.75, or about $1.50 per ounce higher than the entry price, I made a lot of money on the trade.[1] I had 1,200 of the 5,000 ounce contracts, so I made about $9 million on the trade. That was a 45% gain on the account size of $20 million I was trading that year. But I left too much money on the table.

My mistake was that I then viewed trading as a battle of will instead of as a game of finesse. I felt that if I could take the pain of letting my positions go against me, it would make me a better trader.

1. In his book on the Turtles, *The Complete Turtle Trader* (Harper Collins, 2008), and in an article that appeared in the now defunct *Trader Monthly Magazine,* Michael Covel erroneously reported that I lost a large sum of money on this trade. In fact, it was a big winning trade for me.

I should have listened to the advice of Jesse Livermore in his book *How to Trade in Stocks:*

> This incident proves the folly of trying to find out "a good reason" why you should buy or sell a given stock. If you wait until you have the reasons given you, you will have missed the opportunity of having acted at the proper time! The only reason an investor or speculator should ever want to have pointed out to him is the action of the market itself. Whenever *the market does not act right* or in the way it should—that is reason enough for you to change your opinion and change it immediately. Remember: There is always a reason for a stock acting the way it does. But also remember that chances are you will not become acquainted with that reason until some time in the future, when it is too late to act on it profitably.

Whenever the market does not act right—that is reason enough for you to change your opinion and change it immediately.

Silver wasn't acting right. In subsequent years, I learned that whenever a market makes a vertical move, as silver did that year, it ends suddenly. Whenever the market breaks down after going vertical, the move is over. Sure, it might rally again to reach or exceed the highs, but the market is psychologically broken.

I should have exited the trade after the failed rally broke down at the point labeled Optimal Exit in Figure C.1. This was the best position and where a seasoned trader would have exited. I let more than $10 million in additional profits slip by because I did not pay enough attention to my intuition and the soft aspects of trading.

As a Turtle, I overemphasized the logical, systematic methods we were taught. I should have remembered that Richard Dennis himself didn't always trade this way; he sometimes used his intuition to exit profitable trades. Using my whole mind while trading would have made me a better trader.

It is a bit ironic that my trading idol, Livermore, the man whose story initially interested me in the idea of becoming a trader, was one of the first systematic traders who saw the need to follow, not neglect, his intuition. Had I read his story more carefully and not been so overconfident in my own abilities as a trader, I might have noticed the advice he gives (again from *How to Trade in Stocks*):

> During the big Bull Market in the late twenties, there were times when I owned fairly large amounts of different stocks, which I held for a considerable period of time. During this period I never felt uneasy over my position whenever Natural Reactions occurred from time to time.
>
> But sooner or later there would be a time when, after the market closed, I would become restive. That night I would find sound sleep difficult. Something would jog me into consciousness and I would awaken and begin thinking about the market. Next morning I would be afraid, almost, to look at the newspapers. But perhaps I would find everything rosy and my strange feeling unjustified. The market might open higher. Its action would be perfect. It would be right at the peak of its movement. One could almost laugh at his restless night. But I have learned to suppress such laughter.

> For next day the story would be strikingly different. No disastrous news, but simply one of those sudden market turning points after a prolonged movement in one direction. On that day I would be genuinely disturbed. I would be faced with the rapid liquidation of a large line. The day before, I could have liquidated my entire position within two points of the extreme movement. But today, what a vast difference.
>
> I believe many operators have had similar experiences with that curious inner mind which frequently flashes the danger signal when everything marketwise is aglow with hope. It is just one of those peculiar quirks that develops from long study and association with the market.
>
> Frankly, I am always suspicious of the inner tip-off and usually prefer to apply the cold scientific formula. But the fact remains that on many occasions I have benefited to a high degree by giving attention to a feeling of great uneasiness at a time when I seemed to be sailing smooth seas.

I was too interested in the "cold scientific formula" and not interested enough in intuition and the right brain's role in my trading for my own good. Had I stopped to notice, I would have exited the silver trade much closer to the optimal point.

This trade has always stayed in my mind as a warning not to get too sure of myself and not to place too much emphasis on the abilities of my logical mind. I was trying to brute-force my trading, to tough it out better than anyone else. I needed to display the finesse of Juan Fangio; I needed to trade with my whole mind.

I kept this trade in mind years later when, after almost an entire year of bullish movement from a base at 1,250, the S&P reached

1,550 and then had a pullback to below 1,400 in late July and early August 2007. This was the first time in almost a year that we had a significant retracement as the market climbed higher. A few months later, in late September and early October, the market surpassed the July high. Unlike the previous new highs of the run-up from 1,250, the market could not hold the new highs. As Livermore would say, "The market did not act right or in the way it should."

If you look at the weekly chart in Figure C.2, you can see that, on a weekly basis, the market presented a classic rebound swing method short trade.

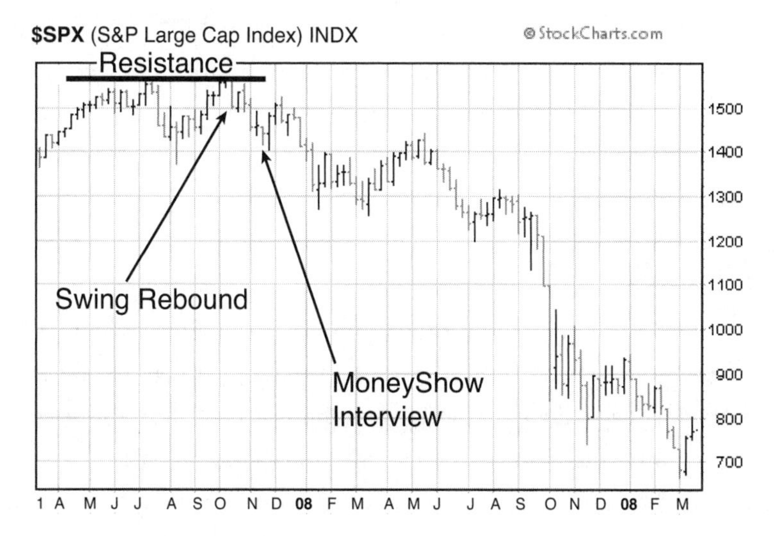

FIGURE C.2 S&P 500 weekly chart

I was recently engaged at the time, and somehow the conversation of the stock market came up with my then future (and now current) father-in-law, who was planning on retiring in a few years. I advised him to get completely out of stocks. It was the first time I had ever advised anyone on their personal investments outside of a professional context. I really hate giving people advice because it is almost impossible to predict the markets. If the market had gone up after that point, I would have put family relations at risk.

This time was different. My intuition was screaming, "Danger!" So I stepped out of my comfort zone and told him what I thought.

At the Trader's Expo a few weeks later, I gave the advice I mentioned in Chapter 1, "The Power of the Gut," when I told the interviewer there was a significant chance of a major down movement. I was thinking of the 1987 silver trade and of Livermore's advice.

So if you find yourself relying on your logic and analysis in your trading, I encourage you to consider the possibility that you are selling yourself short. You could become a better, more complete trader if you develop your whole mind.

Trading as Art

My wife, Jen, comes from a family of artists. She, as well as her mother, father, and brothers, paint and play various musical instruments. They are always working on some project. Jen also loves to go to art museums. We've been lucky enough to have visited some of the top art museums in the world during the last couple of years. I don't come from a family of artists, so this has been something new to me.

One of the more interesting things I've noticed as I've walked the halls of the Prado, the Met, the Van Gogh Museum, and others is the interplay between technique and creativity. The artists I like the best have innovated by taking a technique to a new level, or they have taken a technique that others have pioneered and moved in an entirely different direction. They have combined technique with creativity.

At its best, trading, too, can be an art form.

Anyone can learn the techniques and tools of trading if they take the time to read and practice.

Learning the art of the trade takes a little more effort. It takes a certain willingness to submit to the unknown, the uncertain future, and the danger that might confront you. It takes a willingness to let your intuition drive some of the time. This willingness doesn't come easy to most people. It takes practice.

Start small if you must, but put your intuition to work with actual trades, and you will find that it complements your intellect.

To develop the art of the trade, you need to practice the act of relinquishing some of your decision making to your gut intuition. Only through this practice will you gain enough confidence in your intuition to let it optimally guide you. So start small if you must, but put your intuition to work with actual trades, and you will find that it complements your intellect.

At age 87, after having sculpted *La Pieta* and *David* and painted the Sistine Chapel, Michelangelo scribbled in one of his sketch books "*Ancora imparo,*" which means "I am still learning." The art of the trade is contained in those two words. Make them yours, and you, too, will be able to transform trading technique into art.

AFTERWORD

On Rome, Fishing, and the Upside of "Gut"

"Nothing is more difficult, and therefore more precious, than to be able to decide."

—Napoléon Bonaparte

Rome, more than any other ancient regime, is the model after which we have built modern civilization. The very idea of a Republic with elected representatives comes from Rome. Even the name of one of the houses of the U.S. Congress, the Senate, comes from Rome. The power and extent of Rome's influence has never been surpassed, though some countries—most notably France under Napoléon and Germany under Hitler—have tried.

At the heart of Rome's influence and power lies the innovation in military tactics afforded by its highly disciplined professional armies, the famed Roman legions. Roman military commanders were generally efficient and able men who had served with their troops for many years. The power of Rome was built upon the strength of these men and their legions.

Warfare, especially against a diverse array of enemies, is filled with uncertainty. A commander can never predict exactly what his enemy will do. He cannot predict exactly which of his troops will come under great pressure and falter, or anticipate every surprise and ruse the enemy might throw at him.

Yet military commanders need to make decisions under those circumstances when they cannot be sure what the enemy will do or exactly which course of action will be best under all potential conditions. They must improvise when surprise tactics ruin their plans. They must respond when their lines are broken and their men tire.

They must make decisions.

Fear of Uncertainty

The ability to make decisions under conditions of uncertainty does not come naturally. For most people, making decisions under uncertainty is hard—*very hard*.

When you don't know what the future will bring, normal decision-making skills falter. Human beings are not very good at thinking in probabilities. Uncertainty implies probabilities rather than certainties, so it is hard for most people to make decisions under uncertainty. They can handle logic that says, "If A, then do B," but they can't easily handle logic that says, "If maybe A."

As humans, we have an innate desire to be right. We are programmed to avoid error. So when faced with decisions where there is a significant likelihood that the decision might be wrong, most people freeze. They don't want to make a decision where they might be wrong, so they prefer to not make any decision at all.

Successful trading requires decisiveness. You must be able to pull the trigger with conviction and confidence. You must likewise be able to exit positions when the time is right. Hesitation can kill you. Panic can kill you.

You need to stop analyzing and use your intuition to make quick decisions with imperfect information at hand, knowing that your decision might turn out poorly. And you must do this without losing your confidence when it does turn out poorly.

Most people find this difficult because there is too much pressure on the decision itself. So one way to increase your decisiveness is to reduce the pressure on the individual decisions you make.

One way to increase your decisiveness is to reduce the pressure on the individual decisions you make.

Roman Tactical Lessons

You can learn some lessons about ways to reduce the pressure on decision making from the tactics of the Roman army.

The Roman legions were generally arrayed in four lines: the first in one solid line and the second through fourth in groups known as *maniples*. Each maniple was composed of two centuries each of about 80 men (originally 100 men, which is where we get the English word "century").

The first line was comprised of lightly-armored javelin throwers, known as *velites*. The other three manipular lines would be comprised of standard Roman heavy infantry each equipped with a shield and a short heavy thrusting sword, known as a *gladius*. Unlike the typical enemy that had solid lines, once the velites had retreated, the Roman legions had regular gaps in each line like a checkerboard so the second line backed up the gaps in the first line, and the third line backed up the gaps in the second line. These gaps gave the legions great flexibility in their maneuvering.

To start the attack, the first line, the velites, would throw their javelins at the enemy and then retreat through the gaps in the first regular infantry line. The rear half of each maniple of the second line of regular centurions would move sideways and forward to fill the gaps in the lines, and then the entire line would attack the enemy in a solid unbroken line. The front line would continue fighting until tired, at which point, the third line would move forward to relieve the second line. These two lines would alternate between resting and fighting.

The fourth line was generally held as a strategic reserve that was available to support weak spots in the line or to reinforce the flanks if there was an attack there. This strategic reserve kept the commander from over-committing to any one decision.

The tactical flexibility and maneuverability of the legions allowed the commanders to move troops around to respond to unexpected challenges on the battlefield. It also allowed commanders to reinforce positions opposite weak points in the enemy lines with fresh *shock troops* who were more likely to be able to break through and rout the enemy. By applying these reserves at various points throughout the battle, a commander could experiment to probe for weakness while maintaining a safe level of reserve capability in case of weakness in his own lines.

Finally, the tactical flexibility of the legions and their highly disciplined troops allowed the roman generals to build contingency plans because they knew they could move men around in response to threats as they developed. This meant that early mistakes in their decisions could be corrected in time to prevent a loss of the battle.

Because any mistakes from early decisions could be corrected due to the tactical flexibility of the formation, the discipline of the troops, and the availability of a strategic reserve, Roman commanding generals could be more decisive without endangering their success. This, in turn, allowed them to seize the opportunity when it presented itself.

Pressure Relief

Likewise, in trading or in life, if you reduce the pressure on individual decisions by leaving yourself some tactical flexibility and maneuvering room, you will be able to make those decisions more quickly and with a lower level of emotional anguish. This, in turn, will make room for a more intuitive decision making process, a quicker process, and a more decisive process.

Learning from the example provided by the Roman legions, here are some specific actions you can take to reduce the pressure on individual decisions and increase tactical flexibility:

- **Don't overcommit**—so you don't suffer as much if a decision is wrong
- **Remain flexible**—and adapt your tactics as events unfold
- **Experiment**—to test several ideas to get more information
- **Have a plan B**—to know what to do if an initial decision is wrong

These are all actions that are second nature to a master trader. They are also useful for managing uncertainty outside of the trading context.

High Voltage—Keep Out!

One of my earliest memories is when I was alone in my room as a child and I unscrewed the light bulb and placed a nickel into the light socket. I don't remember why I did this; I only remember there were a lot of sparks, and then the lights went out. My parents came in a few minutes later because they heard the noise and found out what happened. The voltage of the lamp was normal 110 volt U.S. household current. Still, by the standards of the U.S. National Electric Code (NEC), that voltage was not true high voltage.

High voltage, the kind you are warned about in big signs in industrial settings, is defined by the NEC to be voltage above 600 volts. The choice of this particular voltage is not arbitrary. At around 600 volts, air breaks down and ceases to be an insulator at short distances. Sparks jump. Electricity is more dangerous at higher voltages.

Had I been experimenting with true high voltage as a kid, I might be dead.

You can't avoid danger all the time. In trading, you must accept risk to win. But there is no need to deal with high voltage risk that can kill you when the garden-variety kind will meet your needs.

Further, it is much easier to make a decision when you know that if you are wrong it won't kill you. Not over committing in your trading takes the pressure off your decisions and makes it easier for your intuition to shine.

Not over committing in other life decisions also makes it easier to follow your gut.

Whatever May Come

I took classes in Tae Kwon Do a few years back. One of the first things the Tae Kwon Do master taught the students was the basic stances. There is a front stance that is used more for attacking, a back stance that is used for defending, and a sitting stance which is more of a neutral posture. For each of the stances, the master taught us to maintain our body erect so our weight was centered and balanced.

When we were taught punches and kicks, we were taught to punch and then pull our fists back. Likewise we were taught to kick and pull back our legs and feed. The reasons for this became obvious when we practiced against the bags. If you kicked the bag, the force from the kick would throw the bag backward, and it would also throw you backward with the same force. As Newton said, for every action, there is an equal and opposite reaction.

So a kick without a pullback would create a force, while a kick with a pullback lessened the force and made it easier to keep your balance. Likewise, a missed punch by itself would throw you off balance, but a missed punch with a snappy pullback would leave you in perfect balance.

Some years later I moved to Buenos Aires, Argentina and took a series of tango dancing lessons at a studio run by a famous Argentine tango dancing couple, Mayoral and Elsa Maria. Mayoral was a classic old-school tango dancer. He and his wife could move around like they were both connected together only to separate at times and then come back together again like they had been dancing together for almost 50 years—and they had.

With tango dancing, like with Tae Kwon Do, one of the fundamental principles is to maintain your balance. You must keep your center of gravity over the top of your feet so you don't put too much weight on any one foot.

The reason balance is important for both tango and Tae Kwon Do is the same. If you are balanced, you have options. You have the flexibility to move in any direction at any time. If you are off balance, you have fewer options or perhaps only one.

With tango, this can be a real problem because there are two dancers and the steps are improvised. The man almost always leads, so the woman has no idea what the man is going to do at any point until he signals via subtle hand and body movements. If the man is off balance, he can throw the woman off balance. Then while the man might indicate he wants to go one direction or perform a particular step, the woman might not be able to go in that direction or perform that step because her weight is on the wrong foot. So both parts of the pair must keep their balance for the dance to work.

For the woman dancer, when she doesn't know what is coming, balance is key because it leaves her flexible.

Flexibility is one of the most important ways to take the pressure off the decision-making process so you can let your intuition and gut instincts drive more in your decisions. If you are flexible, you can change your plan if things out different than you had hoped. When you know you are flexible ahead of time, this, in turn, makes it easier to make a quick intuitive decision. So you can be more decisive when you are more flexible.

When you know you are flexible ahead of time, this, in turn, makes it easier to make a quick intuitive decision.

Fishing for Reality

My father loved to fish. He wasn't always the best fisherman, but he loved it. So growing up, I learned to fish at an early age, and it was an ongoing feature of my childhood.

Fishing is filled with uncertainty. You never know when a fish is going to strike. You never know when a big fish is going to break your line. You never know when a school of fish that has been biting steadily will stop suddenly.

I learned at an early age that not every cast of the lure results in a fish. Some days you have to cast a lot of times to catch any fish. Some days you can cast all day long, and you won't catch anything at all.

Each cast of the rod is like a little experiment, an attempt to see where the fish are and where they are biting. If you are smart, and your first attempts don't bring any bites, you will alter your technique or the spot you are casting toward ever so slightly to increase the chances that you will find a fish.

In an uncertain world in uncertain times, your decisions are like the casts of a fisherman. You don't know if they are right; they are really experiments—your best guess where the fish might be. If you look at them as experiments rather than *decisions*, it takes the pressure off the process a bit.

This, in turn, makes it a little easier to go with your gut.

Plan B or C

Every experiment can have positive and negative results. It does what you want, it doesn't, or something in between. In trading, knowing ahead of time what you will do if the market turns against you should be part of the plan before a trade is initiated.

This simple practice makes it much easier to make trading decisions. When you have concrete bounds on the worst-case scenario, you know what it will cost to be wrong.

In other areas of uncertainty in life, having a plan B is an effective way of dealing with uncertainty. Developing a contingency plan is a way of acknowledging the reality of the existence of the uncertainty itself. If you don't know what the future will bring, it makes a lot of sense to plan for the possibility that the future brings something other than what you expected or hoped. Uncertainty means that contingency plans are needed.

It is much easier to make a contingent decision. When you have a plan B in mind, it leaves you free to go with your gut.

Less Fear More Intuition

These four means to reduce the pressure on a decision—not over committing, remaining flexible, experimenting, and having a plan B—are also ways of reducing the fear of making the wrong decision.

Less fear makes room for more intuition in your decision making.

In thinking about the benefits of the wind tunnel in training for skydiving formation flying that I described in Chapter 8, "Techno Traders," I left out one important benefit: the reduction in fear.

When you jump out of a plane, you have, at most, 60 to 70 seconds of time before you have to pull your main chute—if you want to leave yourself time to pull your reserve chute in case your main chute doesn't work. If you are working with others, you need to leave yourself an additional 10 seconds or so to allow the group to spread out so each skydiver is at a safe distance from the other divers when their parachutes open. So, you have perhaps 40 seconds in which to perform your actions. If you take too long or find yourself spinning uncontrollably at the wrong time, you might die.

There is always a certain element of healthy fear in the back of your mind as you make maneuvers. That fear disappears quickly once you get inside a wind tunnel and realize that it is a comparatively safe place to practice. With the reduction in fear comes an increased willingness to experiment and to fail. These experiments and failures, in turn, increase the rate at which you learn.

As you begin to feel safe practicing, your conscious mind begins to let go. Your left brain stops wanting to be the safety police. It stops telling you to be, "Careful! Careful!"

As the left brain lets go, the right brain can start to take over. This is the reason that Astrid's game of tag worked so well. When you are playing a game and having fun, you are generally not afraid. So as I chased her around the wind tunnel and lost my fear, I lost the deliberate control I had previously required when performing a maneuver. The reduction in fear allowed me to use my intuition instead.

You don't over commit, so you know a mistake will not be fatal; you remain flexible so you can adapt your approach as reality unfolds; you experiment so you can uncover the best approach; and you have a plan B so you know what to do if you primary plan doesn't work out. If you take these steps, you will have less fear in your decision making process.

Less fear will leave room for greater intuition.

Less fear will leave room for greater intuition.

Take the pressure off. Drop the fear. Learn to let your intuition drive.

Conscious Decision Making

Another way to improve your decisions is to become more aware of the decisions that you do make.

Even though your goal is to make more decisions without using your conscious mind, you need to be conscious of the fact that you are making decisions to improve. So you need to be conscious of the decision-making process and its outcomes but try to use more of your unconscious decision-making skills when making those decisions.

The following example serves to illustrate this point. In his book, *The Power of Intuition*, Gary Klein discusses the development of an intuitive decision-making process for rifle squad leaders within the U.S. Marine Corp. One of the exercises they performed as part of the process was an analysis of the decisions that a squad leader had to make in the course of his duties.

Gary started the process by asking them about the most difficult decisions they had to make over the previous years. In short order they had built a list of 30 decisions. Gary describes the process as being a big eye opener for them because they had always assumed that being noncommissioned officers meant they didn't make decisions but only executed them. In reality, they were making decisions without being conscious of the process behind those decisions. In other words, they didn't realize that they were actually making decisions.

One difficult decision the marines highlighted was the estimation of the time it would take to move their squad from one point to another. The marine said they used a simple formula of 2.5 kilometers per hour to make their estimates. Then they proceeded to discuss the reasons that this simple formula didn't work. It ignored the type of terrain, how much weight they were carrying, whether any of the marines were injured, how muddy the ground was, how careful they had to be to avoid detection by the enemy, and many other important factors. Klein then asked how they trained to make this important decision.

The marines realized that because they hadn't considered these estimates to be decisions, they were not making any attempts to determine the factors that affected the reliability of these estimates. Once they were aware of these factors, they started to train while estimating times using these factors. Over time, they found they could develop an intuitive feel for how long any particular journey including all the factors. They found they could make much better estimates than the 2.5 kilometers per hour they used to use.

The same holds true with many trading and life decisions. Often people will defer their decisions to rules of thumb provided by others or to the advice of experts, not realizing that the act of deferring is itself a decision. This can cause a lot of problems for anyone operating outside their area of expertise. As the rifle squad leaders found out, even a completely intuitive split-second right-brain estimate can be more accurate than a rigidly applied rule of thumb that does not account for the most important factors.

Like the squad leaders with their 2.5 kilometers per hour formula, many new traders use a rule of thumb to determine the risk levels for their trades. For example, they might risk 1% or 2% on a given trade. This approach can be dangerous or far from optimal. By deferring on the analysis and decision-making process, the traders who use these rules of thumb are neglecting opportunities to train their gut. They won't have their intuition honed to adjust for the factors that make trading different sized positions better. So when the markets go crazy, they might end up blindly using their rule of thumb when a more conservative approach is warranted.

A specific example is warranted here. I generally use the volatility of a particular market to determine the risk I use. I use the amount the market moves up and down per day on average to determine how many shares or contracts to trade.

This approach has one drawback. At times the market will go quiet right before an explosive move. The volatility can drop to a small fraction of what it might have been only one month earlier. So you can end up with a position that is a large multiple of what it might have been earlier.

This can work in your favor if the move happens in a controlled fashion. You will have time to get out if the market moves against you.

Sometimes, however, these explosive moves happen overnight when the markets are closed. Or the market moves so suddenly that there is no opportunity to get out at the price you had hoped. When this happens, you can sustain a loss much larger than you expected.

If you blindly follow your rule of thumb, you will end up in trouble in these situations. If you allow your intuition to be your guide, you will find that on occasion, every once in a while, a smaller position size is warranted than your typical size. So allow your intuition to assert a more conservative stance on occasion.

Finally, if you are aware of the decisions you are making, even if you defer to the advice of others, you will still be able to learn and train your own intuition. You can monitor how your intuition fares against the advice of experts even when you follow that advice instead of your own intuition. In this way, you can start to gain some confidence in your own decisions, even outside your own areas of expertise.

Go with Your Gut

My rational mind must concede that it might be an instance of selective memory, but I cannot recall a single instance in my life when I regret having followed my gut instincts when they have been strong.

In stark contrast, I can think of several disastrous decisions I made when my rational mind overruled my intuition.

One particular decision stands out. Shortly after I took Borealis—the software company I started a few years after the Turtle program ended—public, we held a board meeting. At this point, one of our obligations was to appoint two board members who were acceptable to the investment bank that had lined up the investors for the public offering. One of the board members was an easy decision. The other proposed board member was a problem. We had bad blood between us, and we didn't trust each other. I didn't think our small company could afford to have potential conflicts on the board. In my gut, I felt we should ask the investment bank for another prospective member.

I confided my concerns to one of the other board members after the dinner we generally held before our all-day board meetings. He advised me to go with the bank's recommendations. He felt we could work things out. I deferred to his much greater business experience and followed his advice. I regretted that decision from that point forward. I should have listened to my gut instincts.

The battle for control of the company which ensued consumed too much of my time and ultimately led to the destruction of the entire company. I should have listened to my gut.

The intuition can be especially valuable in life as it is in trading. It can help warn of danger, the hidden calamity which awaits. So if your intuition is flashing danger signs about some course of action or some personal relationship, I urge you not to ignore those signs.

If your intuition is flashing danger signs about some course of action or some personal relationship, I urge you not to ignore those signs.

Over time, I've learned to trust my gut more and more, and I've been happier with the decisions I make as a result. I'm sure there is a line out there somewhere that is the point at which I will trust my intuition too much to the detriment of my decision making. The line represents the point of perfect balance of intuition and the conscious logical mind.

I still haven't reached it. I keep finding that the more I learn to trust my gut, the better things turn out.

I hope that as a result of this book, you too will be able to trust your gut so you can learn to use your whole mind in your trading.

And in your life.

Bibliography

Works Referenced

Donaldson, Gerald. *Fangio: The Life Behind the Legend.* London: Virgin, 2009.

Faith, Curtis. *Way of the Turtle.* New York: McGraw-Hill, 2007.

Klein, Gary. *The Power of Intuition.* New York: Currency Books, 2003.

Klein, Gary. *Sources of Power: How People Make Decisions.* Boston: MIT Press, 1998.

Le Bon, Gustav. *The Crowd: A Study of the Popular Mind.* New York: Cosimo Classics, 2006.

Lefevre, Edwin. *Reminiscences of a Stock Operator.* New York: Wiley, 1994.

Livermore, Jesse. *How to Trade in Stocks.* New York: Duell, Sloan & Pierce, 1940.

Ludvigsen, Karl. *Juan Manuel Fangio: Motor-Racings Grand Master.* Somerset, UK: Haynes, 1999.

Mackay, Charles. *Extraordinary Popular Delusions and the Madness of Crowds.* Radford, VA: Wilder, 1841.

Patel, Charles. *Technical Trading Systems for Commodities and Stocks.* Greenville, SC: Traders Press, 1998.

Pink, Daniel H. *A Whole New Mind: Why Right Brainers Will Rule the Future.* New York: Riverhead, 2006.

Soros, George. *Soros on Soros: Staying Ahead of the Curve.* Hoboken, NJ: Wiley, 1995.

Suggested Reading

Conway, Mark R., and Aaron N. Behle. *Professional Stock Trading.* Waltham, MA: Acme Trader, 2003.

Douglas, Mark. *Trading in the Zone: Master the Market with Confidence, Discipline and a Winning Attitude.* New York: Prentice Hall Press, 2001.

Elder, Alexander. *Trading for a Living: Psychology, Trading Tactics, Money Management.* New York: Wiley, 1993.

Faith, Curtis. *Way of the Turtle.* New York: McGraw-Hill, 2007. (Covers position sizing)

Kiev, Ari. *Trading to Win: The Psychology of Mastering the Market.* New York: Wiley, 1998.

LeBeau, Charles, and David W. Lucas. *Technical Traders Guide to Computer Analysis of the Futures Market.* New York: McGraw-Hill, 1992.

Steenbarger, Brett. *The Daily Trading Coach: 101 Lessons for Becoming Your Own Trading Psychologist.* Hoboken, NJ, Wiley: 2009.

Steenbarger, Brett. *The Psychology of Trading: Tools and Techniques for Minding the Markets.* Hoboken, NJ: 2003.

Tharp, Van K. *Trade Your Way to Financial Freedom.* New York: McGraw-Hill, 2006. (Covers position sizing)

Weissman, Richard L. *Mechanical Trading Systems: Pairing Trader Psychology with Technical Analysis.* Hoboken, NJ: Wiley, 2004.

Trading War Stories

Lefevre, Edwin. *Reminiscences of a Stock Operator.* New York: Wiley, 1994.

Schwager, Jack D. *Market Wizards: Interviews with Top Traders.* Columbia, MD: Marketplace, 2006.

Schwager, Jack D. *The New Market Wizards: Interviews with Top Traders.* Columbia, MD: Marketplace, 2008.

Additional Reading

Crabel, Toby. *Day Trading with Short Term Price Patters and Opening Range Breakout.* Greenwood, SC: Traders Press, 1990.

Gilovich, Thomas. *How We Know What Isn't So.* New York: Free Press, 1993.

Pardo, Robert. *Design, Testing and Optimization of Trading Systems.* New York: Wiley, 1992.

Wilder, J. Welles. *New Concepts in Technical Trading Systems.* Greensboro, NC: Trend Research, 1978.

About the Author

Curtis Faith is author of the bestselling book *Way of the Turtle*, which has sold 70,000 copies and has been translated into nine languages. In his early twenties, Faith earned more than $30 million as a member of the legendary Chicago trading group, the Turtles. He has founded several software and high-tech startups, including a public company and an Inc. 500 firm. His most recent book is *Inside the Mind of the Turtles*.

The Art of the Trade Trilogy

In this book, you've learned the trading psychology that helps and hinders whole-mind trading, and you've learned how this knowledge gives you an edge in mastering risk. With this knowledge, I encourage you to test these techniques, document their results, and if you have questions or problems, write back to me at www.curtisfaith.com. One reason I want to hear from you is that I can learn from you. *Trading from Your Gut* is the first in a three-book lineup covering whole-mind trading, and I am excited about learning from the experiences of other traders and investors as I consider the content of the next two books and the related content we'll be positing on www.curtisfaith.com.

The beauty of whole-mind trading is that you can apply it to whatever asset class or investment sector you want; and it can be used to trade accounts of all sizes. Our next book will address Forex trading, where readers will discover how to use the whole-brain approach in the high-risk, high-reward world made possible with the 50:1, or even 200:1, leverage available with a retail Forex trading account. In the third book, our focus will be trading on a shoestring. In these three books, I share my experience in the psychology of trading and risk with every level of trader from active and sophisticated to novice.

The next book on trading foreign currencies (Forex) is of particular interest to me. The currency markets have been the most consistently profitable markets I have ever traded. Earlier in this book I referenced George Soros' reliance on instinct. Soros is arguably the most legendary currency trader in history. Forex markets are one of the few higher-leverage markets available to traders with accounts of all sizes. Forex—a one trillion dollar market—is particularly well suited to whole-mind trading. Whole-mind trading gives you an advantage that will serve you well, whether you are trading with a large or small account.

Some of the topics I will cover in the new book include:

1. **The Business of Brokerage**—Learn how Forex brokers make money and why the decision about which broker to use may be the most important one you will make.
2. **Lessons on Leverage**—Leverage is an important bonus to Forex trading. It offers the ability to earn large returns from a relatively small account. This leverage can come back around to bite you if you don't understand it and pay attention. High leverage is for experts. Learn how to apply the right level of leverage in your trading.
3. **Living with the Big Fish**—The Forex markets are big—so big that even government central banks cannot control the price of their currency. This reality calls for special attention on the part of a Forex trader.
4. **Forex Psychology**—In general, Forex traders are interested in growing their accounts at a faster pace and are less concerned with preserving capital at all costs since there is not much capital to begin with. This makes them vulnerable to certain human psychological flaws that can affect their trading. Learn how to manage your own psychology.

5. **Discretionary or System?**—Included is a discussion of the differences between discretionary trading and algorithmic trading viewed from the perspective of the Forex trader. This will highlight the difficulty of implementing algorithmic trading systems at the shorter timeframes that prove better for Forex traders.

6. **Risking Right**—Too much risk combined with high leverage can decimate a trading account. If you're trading a small account, disaster can come swiftly with as little as one bad trade. The traditional measures of risk may not be appropriate for a Forex trader. Learn how to decide how much to risk on each trade.

7. **The Right Timeframe**—Learn how to decide whether Day Trading, Swing Trading, or Longer-Term Trading is appropriate for you.

8. **Growing as a Trader**—There are better options for traders with larger trading accounts. Learn how to decide when you are ready to make the transition to a different type of retail account and how to adjust your trading to account for these differences.

Index

I

J–K

L

M

U–V

W–Z

FT Press
FINANCIAL TIMES